GW00731511

WHERE GO THE DEAD

An insight into life after life

ANTHONY J MEAD

AMAZON BOOKS

Copyright © 2020 ANTHONY J MEAD

All rights reserved

The characters and events portrayed in this book are fictitious. Any similarity
to real persons, living or dead, is coincidental and not intended by the author.

No part of this book may be reproduced, or stored in a retrieval system,
or transmitted in any form or by any means, electronic, mechanical,
photocopying, recording, or otherwise, without express written permission
of the publisher.
Any attempt to infringe, undermine the authors rights will be met with legal
action. The book is not to be sold or offered as a download other than by the
legal publishers - Amazon Books.

ISBN: 9798649487689

Cover design by: AMAZON
Library of Congress Control Number: 2018675309
Printed in the United States of America

Dedicated - to the loving memory of Agnes Mary Wright.

Roger Hemmings
Jayna Mead
Barbara Fielder

Mona Sedero
Lynne Meason
Roy and Ann Bullock
Irene Muriel Jenking
Dick Jenking
Nellie and Ernie Jenking
Sharon Fowkes and Graham
Dr Rikkin Jethwa, Sita and Family
Whitehouse Dental Surgery Team, Melton Mowbray

To all the FABULOUS NHS staff in the UK and other area's. Also, all Hospital workers in the UK and Carers in Homes and NHS Hospitals staff worlwide.

All dear friends and clients who have consulted me in my apartment over the last forty years.

Anthony.

CONTENTS

MIND. Part 1

INTRODUCTION

For the next seven days, two, weeks, a month, or however long it takes. Imagine you and I sharing the same mind space. Together, a team we share both probability and potential of what happens when a person dies. We study the minds of those about to pass - show the sequence of events souls encounter before entering the realms of spirit.

Discover why some souls gravitate to the earth plane rather than head straight for the spiritual life. We look into the mindset concerning suicide, dispel the myths surrounding it. Tackle non-believers who didn't even know they had gone. Discover dark and empty souls - how to avoid them. And share groundbreaking information regarding higher life vibration while joining forces in understanding the great laws of karma.

Nothing held back - we face it. Together, transcending the powerful laws of the Universe. In unity, friendship, with a common bond for knowledge we discover -

WHERE GO THE DEAD

WHERE GO THE DEAD

A SPIRITUAL BOOK - IT WILL ENLIGHTEN YOU

'Truth creates fear in our lives - simply because
we get used to hearing the opposite.'

◆ ◆ ◆

Anthony J Mead 2020

CHAPTER 1 - WHAT HAPPENS WHEN YOU DIE?

Your soul leaves your body. It gets out. Sometimes, it gets away fast from the corpse. Other times, it creeps or oozes away, which can take several minutes. But parts from the flesh, a body it has occupied for days, years, a lifetime in some instances. Which you can imagine must feel strange. Carry on reading, and I will take you through the whole process experienced by those who make the journey - from the body to beyond.

I will explain the little idiosyncrasies experienced while the transition is underway. You will understand the whole process, start to finish. Reading the book will enable you to conquer the fear of passing over, give an insight into how easy a task life and death turns out to be. Under normal circumstances, we never think about dying. Why should we? After all, life is about living and, while you are alive, you try to live up to the accolade. When you are young it is the last thing on your mind, even in old age we hardly dwell on it, mainly, if we are fit, healthy, and still feel good.

But when people reach a certain point in their lives the question more often than not creeps in. 'When will I die? What will happen to me?' The fact is, no one can give you an answer and be sure the answer is correct - including the author of this book. We can preach all day long from a variety of angles. The truth is though; there is no proof. I have no particular take on the matter that is any better or worse than a million authors before me. But what I have is a set format and plan. Put together over many years of being a psychic and giving readings through the media of *I Ching*. This form of channelling enabled me to form a blueprint of how the life and death process works.

I am going to share the information with you. Tell you everything I know, have channelled over forty years. More important, though, I will let you decide the authenticity of my writing. Your intuitive soul insight can resonate with my work and determine its fate. I always believe that at a fundamental soul level, our intuition knows instinctively - what is good or bad. Read the logic of what I put before you and decide whether or not it grips you from the heart. Connects in such ways as to impress upon the inner you - that it makes too much common sense for it not to be true.

Along with the information, there will be a few storylines to graphically home in on the point. We are all psychic underneath never believe any different. Everyone has this ability. It's just that; some develop it more than others, using it regularly keeps the intuition sharp.

CHAPTER 2 - TWO WAYS OF LEAVING

There are two ways to leave life. In a sense, two ways to pass over. One is what I term an organized death process. This process is where the person reaches a certain age and expires through illness or old age. You do not have to be so far advanced in the sense of ninety-something to qualify. You may be in your thirties, forties, or perhaps fifties and sixties - who knows. Sometimes, even young people go this way. Did not want to die but got ill, and there was no way of being saved.

The other way is what I call, fatalistic death. This way of leaving is where you die suddenly, and it's a shock to all, a sudden, unprecedented heart attack, accidents and even suicides. The main criteria being - you were not expected to leave! In a sense, you went on the spur of the moment, in a flash. Why it is it like this? There are many variables, karma, interference from other people, time, and circumstance. Only the Universe knows.

The two types of death are dealt with separately in the Spiritual Realms. In an organized death process, the souls of deceased family members and the like gather around in anticipation of a passing. In other words, they know definitely, the person is coming across to be with them, so they get ready for it. It's a common occurrence. In hospitals where people lie dying, they often talk to long lost loved ones like mum and dad, other family members who have passed. They even comment to nurses about it while gazing wistfully into the ceiling. This situation is not rocket science. They look up to the sky because this is where they see them - above them, looking down. The souls gather, ready to receive the new arrival, a greeting to the beautiful life that awaits. It is similar to birth here. The Midwife and the family collect, expecting the new-born infant, welcoming them into the world. Passing over is similar; someone meets you, ready for you.

How do they know you are coming over? I can explain it. Because it is an organized type of death, the person ill, deteriorating, heading for the end. They emit signals, picked up in higher life. Souls in the higher dimensions aware, preparing for you to arrive. It's not a quick thing; it takes time but, in a sense, people heading for organized deaths have enough. Plus, those in the higher realms equally have enough time to evaluate the information - prepare for the gathering.

The souls in the higher life have another advantage in being able to pinpoint the exact time (or near it) of a passing. I can tell you how. A fifth-dimensional viewpoint is allowing them a glimpse of the near future. Yes, all souls in the afterlife have an inherent ability to see the near future - **DEFFO!** It does not matter if they were spiritual or not when on the earth plane. The fact that they have passed over gives them an edge. They see the immediate future, and I can prove it or nearly so.

Here is a small analogy that you can think on for a while; it concerns an ant. An ant is a lower life form on this planet. An insect with an insect's viewpoint if you can imagine such a thing. Now, if a higher dimensional life force such as a human being looked into an ant's nest, what would he or she expect to see? Easy, loads of tiny creatures all frantically milling around like idiots doing what? Very little on the surface - *Naff All.* Further examination would possibly see this slug-like thing (queen) just lolling around being an oversized maggot. No seemingly useful purpose and very little going for them. A bit like Prime Ministers question time or a typical day in the House of Lords.

But how wrong can you be? Beneath this milling mass of confusion lies an ingenious plan - the social organisation of an ant's nest, a modern-day miracle of the Universe. You have to be in it to appreciate. There's more though if you and I saw an ant crawl across a desk, and it was heading in the direction of say, a clock. We could both make a realistic prediction regarding when the ant would get there. Give or take a few seconds we would be near as damn it right. The ant, of course, would have no idea about us.

Now, transfer the analogy to spiritual life, and you get an idea of how souls perceive us. And how easy it is for them to make a prediction. I know we are not insects (LOL), but we share traits.

When souls look down, they see us milling around chasing the impossible dream. The souls are aware of our existence; we don't know them. Regarding the near future - they see it.

The other way you can pass is through what we call, fatalistic death - it can be an instant way out, but there are difficulties. When a person dies suddenly, unprecedented, there are no visible signs to alert all the family souls in the higher life. So, they do not always know you are coming over, not entirely ready to receive you. This situation does not mean you die alone. Sentinel Souls patrol the Universe. They know precisely when you go and reach you in an instant. When I say instant, I mean instantaneous. How is it done? The mechanics are not known. But, it's a higher life with a higher vibration, and I can only suggest that it's subtle combinations of fifth-dimensional thinking and soul energy, enabling travel faster than the speed of light. The Sentinel Souls reach you and support your mind regarding passing. In lots of cases, the souls are familiar to you or would have been at some point in your earthly life. And, even if you don't recognize them, there are no worries - you are at ease.

At this point, I need to explain something to you concerning how souls think and feel in the afterlife. The spirit world is collective, group orientated in terms of how souls exist with one another. When I say, group orientated, I don't mean souls are all stuck together in one mighty lump. They live in groups only if they want to. But the point I am making is, they share a collective vibration of wellbeing and support regarding all other souls that have contact with them. In other words, they are positive, enthusiastic, and well-meaning in all facets of soul life.

This mindset influences the overall vibration by creating a *love energy*. Yes, that's right, a love vibration or energy that has tremendous power, influence, and is the fundamental core of life in the higher dimensions. You can imagine how it is when you get conditions such as these - you are happy and bright. Fundamentally, pure light and energy, as innocent as the first day of your creation. Life in the spiritual realms is big, full, pure, and shining.

And what's more, you are safe. In the world of souls, there is no fear. You cannot kill a soul. You cannot harm it or influence it - unless the soul agrees. You can see why messages from higher life all say the same thing. Those passing to the spiritual world do not want to return to the earth plane. They see no reason to come back to a matchbox prison way of life full of pain and hurt.

Yes, In a sense, life on earth is about living in a matchbox, a prison. There is no better way of explaining it. Here we tend not to have the collective or group energy. On planet earth, it's all about being singular - out for us and no one else. Now, don't take offence. There is no personal gripe in the statement. It's purely observational built on fact - we are all party to it. No more so than the author of this book who boasts a multitude of sins. When we come to this life, we don't stand a chance. We cannot be spiritual like those in higher dimensions because we do not have the conditions for it.

Here it's all about survival; people are subject to an array of social, economic, and fear-based nightmares. In the higher realms, it's all about mutual support and love. Here on the earth plane, it's fear, greed, and sometimes murder. Here we close our doors to people because we don't trust them; they can harm us. The essence of our spirituality in this world lies within the deepest parts of our soul - we have to identify, bring and out, and develop it, during the short expanse of time we have available.

FAITH, HOPE, AND CLARITY

In the early part of this chapter, we talked about two ways of leaving life: the organised process and the fatalistic way. People take either one of the routes with a mindset that they are going on to higher consciousness. Even if they didn't think in this way there is usually a resignation to the fact - anything's better than here so we'll keep an open mind.

But some are different. They hold no beliefs within them regarding life after death. People who dogmatically hold to the principle that once dead - that's it, there is nothing. Some swear in the existence of hell, a desolate place somewhere in the Universe full of fire pits and brimstone, screaming souls, and a multitude of evils waiting to devour them. I could spend all day arguing the point - but, it's not worth the aggro. People are entitled to their choice. We all have free will, and you can believe in whatever you choose to, no one can argue against it.

Simply, because, there is no proof either way. So, what do you imagine happens when a person holds such dogmatic views? Refusing to believe that the soul lives on fearing, they will end up talking to the Devil. The answer, not quite the drama we imagine. But a semblance of your beliefs manifesting, taking you to a place resembling all the weird and wonderful things you carried around in your head for donkeys years. So, the guy who thought there was no heaven, only hell, could end up in a situation resembling it, or symbolic of it. In the next chapter, you will meet a man who did precisely this - went around with an archaic, dogmatic, viewpoint regarding what happens once the life is over. Enter Albert Bert Brown the Non-Believer.

THE AGNOSTIC

Albert Brown was a brilliant guy who people knew as Bert. He died in 2010 aged 68 years old. Bert was a real old English, salt of the earth Yorkshire Tyko. He lived and worked in Sheffield where he had a job in a local foundry making steel brackets. You could not have met a better bloke than him. Married with two daughters he was loyal to his wife and a brilliant dad to the two girls who he worshipped from the floor upwards. They in turn along with Bert's wife Annie loved him to bits - he was a fantastic, honest, hardworking, Englishman with one glaring blip on his CV of life. He was totally agnostic. He didn't believe in God, Universe, or the spirit world; he scorned it. "What the bloody hell yer talking about? There ain't no God and no bloody afterlife. When yer dead yer gone, that's it kaput. Hey, life's a joke then yer croak. Anyone who thinks different is a silly old bugger."

I suppose he's got a point there. After all, no one can prove it. But Bert's thinking was not always on this level. Son of a Presbyterian Preacher his upbringing a godly one. Then when he was seventeen years old tragedy struck twice in the space of a fortnight. First up, his dad got hit by a train and died instantly. Then a week later, his mother fell off a chair and banged her head. Two hours later, she died of a brain haemorrhage. This tragedy was enough to prove to Bert that God or a higher life had no part to play in his thinking, and he didn't want to believe in them. "The arseholes in the higher life don't exist, or they wouldn't have taken mum and dad like that. By heck lad yer no be fooling Bert Brown with yer bollox. Stick them, whoever them are, God, the Angels, and the afterlife somewhere the sun don't shine. I believe in Bert Brown - no one else." Says he laughing away like a gormless parakeet chewing a cashew nut..

Mmmm, Mr Angry showing dogmatic views regarding life and death. Nothing gonna change him though, he's like this a stubborn old bonehead. But something did change, a drama, a tragedy, an unrequited piece of fate - guaranteed to decimate twenty boxes of Kleenex super strength. One morning just after he'd got up, Bert Brown collapsed and died of a heart attack. The girls found him propped up against the dining table two lumps of Shredded Wheat sticking out his mouth and a petrified mass of condensed milk froze to the chin. They knew there was something wrong after noticing - he hadn't drunk his tea.

Bert is dead but guess what? He doesn't know it. No clue, never felt better. His feeling, one of massive strength and boundless energy. Also, he seems to be able to think of a thousand things at once. Plus, a sense of total freedom - the will to do whatever he wants. Funny, he thinks, all seemed to start when I tripped just before breakfast. Amazing what a stub of the toe can do - jolts your brain (LOL) brings the old memory back. If it had not been so tragic a circumstance, then the whole thing could be seen as comical.

I'm Gonna pose as psychic fly on the wall here, get involved, enlighten the clown. "Your dead Bert. The toe stub was a massive coronary; it shot you out your body like a bullet from a Bren Gun! You're gone old fruit - you can't even guess."

Bert Brown is dead yet is the last one to know. So, what is he doing? Well, he's leading his life, doing all the things he has become familiar with over the last forty-odd years. Like catching a bus to work, coming home, digging the garden, getting into bed by 9 pm. But how? How do you supposedly drop dead and then continue with all the same nine till five garbage as if nothing has happened? It's a difficult one I agree but will try explaining. There are several reasons why Bert's death affected him (or didn't if you get my drift) the way it did.

For a start, he's agnostic - a non-believer. No faith in God or trust in higher forces. In a sense, death does not exist. His mind continually nags him to conclude there is no such thing - no consideration. Bizarrely, he thinks he can live forever. So, when he did die, he missed it. Missed his own funeral because to him it never happened. Bert thought he had slipped, a momentary jolt, toe stub. Laughable, yes! But it happens a lot, giving one piece of vital information - passing is easy. So seamless, we don't always know it - fools you. When Bert caught his toe, tripped a bit, he experienced a massive heart attack that took him out. Dead instantly, in a second.

It can and does happen - you pass, don't realize. The fatalistic death process, so quick, so easy, you end up missing your big day in the crematorium so to speak. Bert didn't feel a thing, the reason he could not consider that he was dead. In his mind, he was waiting for a big bang that never came - it didn't happen. I feel there is a massive point to argue here. People fear to die, they fear it, and they worry. But there is no need. You virtually walk out your body, or in Bert's case, get thrown out. There's no pain barrier to go through, no terrible circumstance to face. The whole process of passing is pure bliss, enlightening as you can get. It's the life that causes hardship. Pain, suffering, worry, and anxiety, all earthbound traits - they do not exist in the higher consciousness.

Back, then, to our storyline concerning old Bertie boy. A month in earth time has gone. I use the terminology earth time and will explain more of this later. For now, though, thirty days are history, and Bert is dust to dust, blindly attending his own funeral - failing to recognize who he is or rather was. He's getting on with life, but from the soul's perspective, how is he feeling and thinking?

Well there are subtle changes; one of them is time. I will explain, give a breakdown. When you pass, go into a higher vibration, which happens as soon as you exit your body - *the time changes*. Now I am not a maths genius or nuclear physicist. So, can only give a bare outline. I don't want to get deep in the subject or risk an argument with *Albert Einstein* when I eventually go over. *The time in Bert's dimension goes fast - in our life, it's slow*. Bert can imagine five minutes ticking by - here it's a month.

Sounds complicated, not easy to grasp, so don't try. Just simplify, and bear in mind that Bert's time is faster than ours. It produces subtle effects that sensitive souls pick up on. But Bert Brown is not sensitive. He's carried his thick-skinned attitude into the higher life. The mindset just the same as it was here - stubborn, closed. In other words, he thinks no different to when he was alive and in a physical body.

Time is racing, Bert going with it, grinding out life with a daily routine. Doing all the things he did when alive, getting into bed at night with the wife, catching the same bus to work in the morning. Not once does it occur that something is wrong. A period of time passes, perhaps a few months on the earth plane. Ever so slowly, something starts to stir in Bert's thinking. It's not a mega change more, a subtle shade of difference to how he perceives things. For starters, Bert is getting slightly bored. The feeling, one of isolation, loneliness, no one makes time. Annie, the girls, he talks to them every day. The response, like watching paint dry. They hardly seem to care, kind of look through him. Going to work on the bus, the passengers, sitting, staring into oblivion - a depressed bunch. No one says good morning, good evening, kiss my arse or what! The job in the metal works - they all seem preoccupied. The euphoric surge Bert feels about his energies begins to pale. Of course, being a pure light-bodied soul stops out and out depression, not applicable to those who pass on. But it's not exciting, and what's more, he can't work it out. Why is he feeling so flat, so unnoticed, so alone? He won't have long to suffer in silence.

THE ANSWER ABOUT TO MANIFEST WITH

MINDBLOWING CONSEQUENCES!

One morning while Bert sits on the bus, totally alone, locked in thought. He notices something different. In front, on the next seat, there is a man with his back to him dressed in army uniform. He was drawn to the uniform more than anything because it belonged to the Tank Corps. He'd served in the same unit, out in the Middle East during the 1960s. So more out of curiosity than frustration Bert taps the man on the shoulder intending to have a conversation - anything to kill the bloody sheep counting syndrome. The man turns around looks at him, starts smiling. "Hello Bertie," he says. Bert, gobsmacked, momentarily hesitates. "Well bugger me, it's Ernie, Sergeant Ernie Hines, 5th division, Aden, 1967. Bloody hell I'm so happy to see you - I'm dying of boredom." Ernie Hines smile deepens; he grips Bert by the hand in a warm embrace.

The conversation continues. "Ernie I ain't see you for years. I heard you were dead." Ernie running his hand through his hair makes a wry grin - "Bertie, I am dead. And guess what mate - so are you." Bert Brown's mouth became agape, like a Venus Fly Trap without any flies in it. "Gordon Bennett your bloody joking, how did it happen? How, Ernie?" "You collapsed, thought to yourself it was a slip, you had a massive heart attack. Killed you quicker than those sand snakes you used to pop off in the desert."

Bert looking pensive before he speaks. "Explains it, the silence, the lack of conversation. The funeral we went to, bloody hell I get it now. I wondered why they were all crying over someone they didn't know. But they did know didn't they - it was me?" Ernie nods. "Yes, Mucker it was you. We couldn't tell you straight the way, had to get you at this position before breaking the news."

Bert looking slightly confused. "What now, what do I do now?" Ernie's trademark smile blossoms. "Come with me Bertie; I'm going to take you home. You don't belong here anymore, and they're all waiting for you, all the boys, your mum, she can't wait to see you again." Bert's energies seemed to galvanize, he grins, looks wistful. "What about Annie, the girls, I hate to leave them." "I know you do. I know, but you have to let go - at least for a while. They will be alright. There is a tremendous amount of love and respect for you Bertie. They will hold on to it for as long as they live. So, in a sense, they still have you. The essence of you continues on in their hearts. And when they finally step into the light, you will be there waiting to greet them. There's enough love in you to build each a row of houses, one for every day of the week. But, more about this later. Come now, we have to leave. There is so much to do, such a lot to learn. So many things to tell you."

It's not clear what happens next except the bus they are travelling on seems to fill with bright light, then nothing. The two souls vanish, disappear into the rarefied atmosphere. If you had looked up to the heavens that night, you might have seen two shooting stars race across the skies - it's an everyday occurence.

CHAPTER 3 - INNER DETACHMENT

How does the soul leave the body? It's a valid question, and one where not enough information is available. In terms of, the actual process of leaving, getting skimped, ignored, fudged over. In this chapter, I'm going to tell you in orderly stages how the soul departs and moves on. First, though, let me go over a point I made earlier regarding the method of detachment. Souls tend to either shoot from the body quickly or slowly ooze away. I will explain it. A quick demise from a heart attack sees the soul bullet out the body as if shot - instantly. A person dying of cancer in a hospital can get in and out of their skin several times before the final exit. The process can take minutes, hours, even days and weeks before a definitive conclusion.

But as men and women, we need to know what happens when we leave. What is the final process? How does it feel? In the case of a quick exit, sometimes nothing. In the sense of, you don't feel much; the earth hardly moves, you are not aware. In the last chapter, I explained through the media storyline concerning Bert Brown. He did not feel anything, just a trip, foot stub, slight falling. He was never initially aware he'd experienced a massive heart attack and died.

A person lying in a hospital ward, getting ready, experiences more because of awareness, sensing something is going to happen. Though not in every situation, some people drifting in and out of a coma. No time to think or identify with life.

The end of life can happen in stages. One of the first alerts regarding people passing is that they start to see deceased family and friends. As I mentioned earlier, people appear in the ceiling. Older people not far from death often report that they have spoken to their Mother or Father. You get a lot of this, and I don't believe people give it enough credibility. But it should be taken seriously, it ought to be trusted. In a lot of cases, people dream of relatives just before passing. Their recollection of the dream can be vivid, life-like, it's as if they were there with the person having a chat. All of what I am telling you is not classified information - instead, pure soul energy logic, understandable in every conceivable way. Souls gather around; they get ready to receive the new arrival. Indoctrinate them into the higher life, embrace and welcome them.

Another clear indication of the end being in sight is something to do with temperature - it gets freezing. Usually, the sick and ailing person will ask for an extra blanket. They suddenly start to feel immensely cold, yet the room is average temperature or even warmer. Again, not unusual, it happens a lot. As the soul gets near to passing, it gets closer to the spirit world. This closeness of worlds is why the room goes icy for them. The vibration of the spiritual life is coming nearer, getting ready for the crossover. The higher world is cold.

Though, only, to those who are not in it. As a soul in a higher dimension, you feel completely at ease with the temperature, perfect for you. When you're in the earth life and come in contact with the higher vibration, it feels deathly freezing. People who report seeing ghosts in this life will often remark how cold and shivering the experience. We have all heard the saying: - *'someone just walked over my grave.'* 'Someone's just talked about me - I'm all a shiver.'

How do you detach? What do you feel? In the sense of, how does the soul separate from the body during death? For the soul to leave the flesh, it has to do three things. Rise, detach, break free. The soul connects to an invisible cord, similar to the umbilical cord attaching you to your Mother at birth. In this instance, the cord or silver cord as it is known is not visible to the naked eye. Only souls in the higher realms see it. It breaks, allowing the soul to leave the earth body. When the cord first starts to break, it makes a subtle cranking, clicking, sound that under normal circumstances cannot be heard. But, Sensitives, Psychics, can listen to it if they tune in. When the silver cord breaks, it's the end you cannot go back to the body; it's physically impossible.

To recap:

1 - The soul rises out of the body.

2 - Breaks away from the invisible silver cord.

3 - The soul is free to travel in the higher ascended dimension.

A lot of times you see this scenario unfolding. People starting to detach, rise, gripping the sides of the bed. Study close, and you can see the fear in their eyes. For a while, the gripping sustains itself; the fear keeps the soul anchored to the body. But it will not last. You do it a few times; you get away with it. Eventually, though, your mind gets distracted - **'HOOTS MON YOUR SOUL IS GONE,'** up in the air looking down at a corpse, distraught family and friends surrounding it. A lot of new souls desperately try to re-enter the body. As already stated, it's an impossible task. Once the cord snaps, you leave forever. You can never go back to the body you just vacated. Universal law prohibits it.

Which makes one wonder why the soul would want re-entry. I think it's a habit, use, years spent in the same old skin - a bit like a house. You leave a house suddenly after say, sixty, seventy, even eighty years you can forgive yourself for wanting to step back through the front door one more time. We are all different with viewpoints that range from the sublime to the ridiculous. But this is what makes us so special. Human diversity of character, as unique as the Universe we depend on for our needs. In the next storyline, an elderly lady who secretly wanted death but had reservations.

DOUBTING MARY - THE MAGIC CARPET RIDE

The scene is a small cottage hospital in the vicinity of West Heath, Birmingham. In a small private room just off the central ward a woman in her early nineties slowly fades. Enter, *Agnes Mary Wright* or Mary as she likes to be known. Mary is quite a spiritual girl, always was even as a child. Curious rather than active in the work she sought recourse to higher life values all her life. Never in doubt that there was more to living and dying than ordinary folk understand. Now, slowly, she is ebbing, and much to her regret nagging doubts invade her mind. Next to Mary's bed, her son Archie, composed, serious, head slightly bowed. Unlike him, he usually displays a keen wit and laughing nature. Today though, Archie knows his Mother is not long for this life - only a matter of time. He knows she cannot carry on; her spirit is draining out. A far cry from days past when Mary travelled on a train, Birmingham New Street to Melton in Leicestershire, a day spent with 'her Arch' as she calls him. They would meet in a small hotel, take late lunch, afternoon tea, put the world to rights. Mary would then head back to Brum on the train, Arch waving her off on the station platform. The ritual continues for years until Mary broke her hip. From this point, downhill all the way until we get to where we are now.

It would be wrong to suggest Mary is afraid. The spiritual side of her too strong to be doubted, but she worries, anxious about her passing, it's close, she feels it. *What will the end be like? Will I blackout she says to herself? Or will there be a form of choking, fighting for breath, the pain of clinging to what little piece of life I have left?* Opening her eyes, she turns to her son and whispers, "Arch, I'm cold. I'm so cold." "I will get a blanket," says Arch. "Nurse can Mother have a blanket she's feeling the chill." The Nurse gets extra bedding, but Mary still feels the cold. "Unusual," says the nurse. "It's blindingly hot in here the heating is full on."

All of a sudden Mary is aware of something within her. The strangest feeling ever experienced in all her ninety-plus years. It is if she is kind of lifting, rising, and elevating most unusually. No pain or discomfit. The feeling, one of euphoric bliss. Then her mind speaks. Oh, my goodness, I feel a bit lightheaded. She reaches out her hands, one in the direction of Arch, the other firmly to hold to the side of the bed. "What is it, mum?" says Arch. "What's wrong?" "I don't know dear" she whispers. "I feel weightless." Arch holds her hand. "Just rest, mum, try and relax." Mary closes her eyes, and all of a sudden, hears her Mother's voice.

"Agnes what the bloody hell are you doing? Come on; we are waiting for you. Come on; dear throw yourself out of your body. It's easy like the day you swung between those two bloody trees in the garden and tore your frock to shreds - ha, ha, ha." Reality returns, the room still in one-piece Arch and the nurse looking at her. It might have continued, but in the end, it is Arch who signals the final chapter. Gripping his Mothers hand, he whispers in her ear. "Don't be afraid, mum. You can go. It's ok you can leave now. It will be alright." Mary relaxes, the tightness easing, there is an unusual clicking sound like the ticking of a digital clock. She opens her eyes and finds herself looking down at a prostrate body in a bed. Arch holding a corpse-like hand, the nurse, running around frantically trying to rouse a doctor. It is over, painless, gravity-defying, totally blissful - like a magic carpet ride on a *starry sky's Arabian Nights Tale.*

What can we deduce about Mary's demise? - it was painless, nothing to it. The minute she stopped worrying she went, passed seamlessly. Her soul elevating; the silver cord breaking away. She starts to feel relaxed in herself and crosses over. The whole experience euphoric as opposed to being hard and painful. Of course, Mary was not dreadfully ill before she went. She died of old age more than anything else. For a lot of people, it is different; they are sick, leading up to their death. The point to make, though is this: There is nothing to fear about leaving life. You suffer on the earth plane, but in a higher vibration, you bask in a welter of powerful soul energy and spiritual wellbeing. You vibrate at a higher level than you could ever achieve in this world.

CHAPTER 4 - THE REMAINERS

Not every soul leaves the earth life ultimately. In terms of, aspires to the higher realms. Some souls, after they leave, stay around the planet. Similar to the story concerning Bert Brown. But, with subtle differences. In Bert's case, he didn't realise he was dead until a friend appeared and enlightened him. Some souls know they have passed but don't want to do anything about it or go anywhere. These souls gravitate close to the people they love, wives to husbands, children and family in general. Souls do this for a short period; others extend it, for longer. They do it because they have free choice in the Universe.

You do not have to conform to a particular pattern, trend, if you want to stay on the earth after death, you can. Usually, there are more heartfelt reasons than just hanging around with no particular purpose. Some souls cannot bear to leave loved ones - the loved ones left behind do not want them to go. Where the bond between man and wife is so strong, the departed wife or husband stay in the house - cling to their old life while existing in an enlightened state. It is easy for people to have difficulty in understanding the fundamentals of how it happens and why! Before we get to the root of it, i want to talk to you about the higher life.

In the higher life, it is group orientated or collective. Which does not necessarily mean people always live in groups. They can if they want to, but equally, they can be on their own - its free choice. The group or collective orientation works through a supportive, benevolent, vibration which produces universal wellbeing or love consciousness. I will explain in detail. In the higher life, the souls exist in a collective state of wellbeing and camaraderie. They are positive, not negative; they don't damn you. In a sense, they love you. Which does not mean they go around clutching violets and whispering heartfelt, sweet nothings to all and sundry - it's not slush. Instead, universal wellbeing that promotes you rather than puts you down. In the higher life souls create and exist In pure love energy. They never get depressed; they are always on a high. Bad traits cannot exist.

For a start, there is no jealousy. All souls are equal and can-do stuff, get things they need. They do it through universal manifestation. Yes, all souls are equal, but, some more than others because of their advanced spiritual development. This development does not mean that you have to do readings or be psychic to qualify. It's more to do with how you feel about others - your universal mindset. In the higher realms, you accept that some souls are more advanced, you get on with it - it does not make you feel bad. Souls cannot harm you, disfigure you, or kill you. You can kill a human being, but you cannot eliminate a soul. Souls are helpful, supportive, positive, and full of good feeling towards all others, in a sense perfect. In the spiritual life, we can all achieve by getting what we need - there is **NO FEAR!**

Now compare it with this plane of existence - no comparison. Here there is fear by the bucket loads and equal amounts of murder to go with it. Here, people do not like you. A harsh comment and of course, not credible in all walks of life. *Yes, people do love you - lots of them.* But, by the same token, people **HATE** and it's no good pretending it doesn't exist. People are cynical, not supportive - they can't stand you progressing, having more than they do. On the earth plane people cannot evolve in the same collective, group orientated environment like they do in the spirit world.

Why not? There are too many material circumstances creating barriers. For example, under normal realistic conditions, you couldn't invite a hundred people to stay with you for a month in your house. Apart from the apparent size issue, there would be other problems. You could not afford to feed them. It would cost a fortune, economics not practical. Because this is a fear vibration, it influences us into not trusting people. Ten of your hundred guests might steal from you - another barrier.

In the spiritual life, you could ask a hundred strangers to your home. Nothing to stop you, no restrictions. No money needed, or hard work in setting it up. **NO FEAR.** In the vibration we exist, it's about being selfish - we have to be, we haven't got a choice. We have to think of ourselves and our own.

It makes us singular in our outlook, not group orientated like the higher life. In the higher consciousness, there are no apparent barriers. Here there are plenty, this is the difference. But, don't feel bad over it we are all in the same boat, not ready for the higher vibration, not yet. One day it will come, and we will be prepared, all forty trillion of us to quote a figure of speech. We can only do our best. We can only aspire to a higher life by about ten per cent. So, don't try. Don't try to be all spiritual when you need to be material. Think of it, evolve naturally in the confines of what you can realistically achieve.The higher life is a collective love vibration - we know it. Which brings us back to a question posed earlier about souls who choose to remain close to loved ones after passing, rather than move on. Because the higher vibration is love orientated you aspire to it the moment you leave your body. In the sense of once you die the higher vibration kicks in and you become part of it. In fact, you depend on it.

So, why would souls want to gravitate around people who are still living? When they can be a party to the higher love energy available in the spirit world. The answer is this: They gravitate to the people who loved them when they were alive and still love them - because those people drip-feed them. Sustain them with their own personal love energy - make them happy. In a sense oxygenate them but its not oxygen - it's love.

They nourish them with love, straight from the mind and memory bank. The massive, love, respect, emotional pride you feel in those who have gone pings off you as spent, energy, atoms, every second of the day. So, you are feeding them, sustaining them, keeping them with you. You are drip-feeding them pure soul love energy, and they are happy to take it. They are happy to take it because this is what they depend on for their continuing existence.

We can assume it's not totally the same as the higher realms offer. But, human beings, soul energies, go through a lot to stay with those they adore. Think about it, you don't have to be Einstein. In a sense, it's like giving someone life assisting energy. Sustaining them, protecting them, loving them - keeping them with you forever. Or, at least until you go!

BABY SOULS - TRAGEDY OF NOT BEING BORN

During the last forty years, people have come to me for I Ching readings, and I give them predictions. Sometimes in the horoscope, I touch on something emotional, heartfelt, tragic. Other times people come and speak about specific problems, situations in their lives that need looking into. One of the biggest tragedies, women who have lost unborn babies. It's a terrible and sad situation, and I confess to the fact that long after the reading, I have trouble coming to terms with it. So in this chapter, I want to talk about something in the spiritual sense that can offer a little solace and relief. It is not easy to explain and will not take away the pain of losing the precious gift of new-born life - but we have to try.

There is a saying in the I Ching that makes a lot of universal sense. *You can't lose what's really yours even if you throw it away.* It would be easy and understandable to think that when an unborn baby is lost, possibly through some complication - the child is gone forever. Spiritually, though, it has not, and I will try and explain why.

There are two distinct scenarios. If the baby is lost at an early stage in the pregnancy, possibly through miscarriage. Then it can be that a foetus rather than the full soul of a child is lost. This is because, from a higher spiritual viewpoint, the whole, quickening, life-giving energy (soul) does not always enter the foetus until just before birth. The channellings I have received point to six-eight weeks before conception. It cannot be categorically proved but is at least worth considering. The other scenario this: If the child complete with ensoulment dies in the womb, then it still gravitates to the Mother spiritually. In fact, stays connected through the invisible silver chord, enshrining soul energy to the physical body. I explain further.

We know from the previous discussion in this book that the soul is connected to the body by an invisible silver chord. The chord breaks at the point of physical death, allowing the soul to be released. When an unborn child dies in the womb, the silver chord does not entirely cut off. In terms of break away completely. In a sense, part of it does, but there is still a link, channel, connecting the baby to Mother. Instead of the child gravitating to the Mother's womb, it attaches to her mindset. The unborn infant becomes like a symbolic, seed pod attached to Mothers mind and memory.

It retains a karmic bond that lasts throughout the life of the Mother and beyond. Until such a time when it can be born again. This will be in a later karmic incarnation, another lifetime. The child, though, is not lost, not gone away. It is still your baby and, in a sense, stays with you waiting for the right moment in time. May sound fantastic but if you think about it, fits in with the universal way of doing things. Nothing wasted, nothing lost, everything a place and a purpose in the greater scheme.

Some schools of thought suggest the unborn child will grow to adulthood in the higher life. The channellings received through the I Ching dispute some of it. If a child is born and lost at an early age, it grows to full maturity in the higher realms. But if it is an unborn child then in a sense it can hardly develop - it has to be born before it can mature. Without conception, there is no growth. But, and this is where it gets complicated. It may not grow like a baby would grow in earth life. But will develop further in a pod-like state within memory and mind of the Mother.

For a start, the seed of the unborn child takes on all the Mothers pain, anxiety, concerning the loss of life and reconstitutes into something symbolically tangible. Breaks down the Mothers agony and develops it into a character trait. In a sense, totally aware of everything that happened and is happening, preparing for the future. A future that might be anything up to a thousand years away. Or whenever the Universe decides along with your cooperation to bring you back. Reincarnation into a time where the gift of a new-born will be given and not taken away. A time when we make it work for us. How will this reflect later when the child is finally born?

Here are some considerations for you to ponder over.

Don't be surprised to see a child in the future clinging to the mum like she was gonna disappear at any minute. Don't be gobsmacked to see this type of love and loyalty. Don't get shocked when you see a close bonding that borders on the abnormal. And don't be amazed when the little boy or girl gets immediately upset when the mum starts to cry or show her emotions.

And if it's only one child in a family or Mother, Son, or Daughter on their own without the dad - don't be surprised. Sometimes only two or three souls can occupy a particular space - no room for anyone else. Too much lost time to make up, group activity won't work. Try and understand what's going down here. Traits born in the womb under dire pre-life circumstances - made up to you through a kind and caring Universe and a little piece of heaven, your special baby. Who in a funny and bizarre sort of way knows what you went through and is trying to love you better. A small story gives more of a graphic description.

INTERVAL

**COMING UP A SMALL STORY, GIVES A MORE
GRAPHIC DESCRIPTION READ ON -**

WE HAVE LIFT OFF HOUSTON..

Once upon a time in a deep, dark, gut-wrenching location. Two figments of somebody's imagination converse quietly. "Seed, listen carefully," says Stamen. "The chances of Pod winning his case are mighty slim." Of course, a lot depends on your testimony when you take the stand." The Seed looking dismayed. "Is it necessary Stamen - taking the stand that is? I mean, I was here six hundred years ago and gave a mighty fair account of myself to both judge and jury. All to no avail, but the testimony is on record. I should not have to go through it all again, surely. And it's damaging for Pod." Stamen grimaced behind plastic-looking frames. "Its necessary Seed because it's the law - a request for conception received. It has to go through a judge and a panel.

There is no way out."

Suddenly, a knock at a door, enter a diligent young spunk bubble eager to please. "Mr Stamen, the case has been brought forward, and the Judge requests your presence at court on Monday morning." The bubble retreats as quick as it floated in. "There," says Stamen. "Not so bad considering, case gonna be solved quicker than we thought." Seed, quick on the draw. "The whole thing should have solved itself weeks ago we're well behind schedule." "Don't worry Seed, says a grinning Stamen, nothing to pay whether it goes overtime or not - it's all on vitamin aid. Copious amounts of it. All governmentally backed or so I've heard - the Mother ship works for the civil service."

The courtroom is jam-packed, a critical case this. On the left-hand side of the room, Pod sat with his Lawyer Stamen. To the right sat a jury - twelve fortified bubbles - twelve good floating orbs dying to do their duty. Just behind Pod and Stamen the opposition - Pistil, a right hardened nut of a barrister. And just behind him was the Seed looking anxious and slightly nervous about taking the stand. "All rise for the Judge," says the court usher. Her Honor Judge Seiravo. *Case 12360x.* The inner versus the potential outer."

Judge Seiravo speaks her first words. "Your call Mr Pistil." "I request Seed to take the stand, your Honor," replies Pistil, a real weed of a guy with a sharp face and hooked nose plus an antagonising brand of dialogue. "Seed Is it not right that on your last attempt some years back you caused untold damage to a tube while travelling through the zone of Fallopia? ""Objection your Honor." Says Stamen. "Seed was never charged with this offence - the opposition is seeking unfair advantage based on hearsay."

"Sustained." Says Judge Seiravo. "Change the angle of attack Mr Pistil." "Your Honor", nods Pistil. "Seed is it not a fact that you have no power in your gun so to speak - no lead in your pencil.? Cannot do the job that you've been commissioned to do. Is it not evident that you are a fraud, cheating the state out of untold amounts of vitamin aid? Is this not so Seed? " The Seed looking down, but not out. "Not true, there was an unrequited blockage in the zonal area

- a tear. Pod thought it might repair itself, so the Bubbles and I continued on the tube. As optimistic as hell I might add." Before Pistil can respond, Judge Seiravo stands up waving her arms. "Vitamin aid coming in - **BLOODY NORAH** loads of it." Recess for lunch." "All rise." Says the Usher.

Mmmm, perhaps at this point you could be forgiven for being slightly dismayed. But look here, it's not every day you get a case like this. Copious amounts of freebie vitamins all paid for by the Mother ship - these lawyer boyo's as much as anyone in life demand their fair share. Or in this instance a good long look at the menu - wheeeeeeeeee!

Four hours later, after some healthy victuals and a bit of digestive wind snoring - the case resumes. This time it's the turn of Pod to be in the dock, cross-examined by his legal representation In the shape of Stamen."Pod what did you do once you realised the damage in the tube area was not going to repair on its own?" I acted out of protocol", says Pod. "I sent significant mind signals to the Mother state regarding how this situation we had encountered might cause termination."

"So," barks Stamen. "You acted out of total good faith and honesty of application regarding informing the Mother ship her universal rights on conception as it stood, this moment in time." "Objection your Honor butts in Pistil. "He's mollycoddling his client in front of the jury." "Overruled Mr Pistil, the jury consist of twelve good Spunky Bubbles." Those twelve honest Bubbles will absorb the information based on the facts - not necessarily the veneer that goes with it - strike on."

Stamen continues his line of questioning. "So Pod, everything then was done to ensure the best possible outcome - conception. But, embryonically speaking you and your team prepared the Mother state for all eventualities?" "Yes, we did." Says Pod. Stamen turned to the jury with a sombre look on his face. The twelve honest Bubbles equally earnest in listening to what he is preparing to say.

"Members of the Jury, it is easy to see in this case that everything my client did regarding the handling of this particular situation was foot perfect and correct so to speak. The reasons behind termination were nothing to do with my client's lack of effort and protocol. But more to do with the conditions of the tubes in Fallopia. Especially the rent or tear that Seed and his team tried to surmount - to no avail. The circumstances just too difficult."

"My client did everything he could to safeguard the Mother state regarding future conception. I, therefore, ask for an immediate acquittal and a karmic time order to come into effect. I also appeal to the courts for the time order to consist of an exceptional stay of residence concerning the whole team. The particular order takes into account costings - to be shouldered by the Mother state and a varied amount of Governmental backup. The outer woman is a civil servant." With that, Stamen and Pod sit down and allow the opposition to have their say.

"Members of the jury," says Pistil. "I am looking for a complete reversal of the karmic order. Pods team acted totally out of hand. Possibly because of desperation regarding vitamin aid for Pod. I also believe that Seed was inept In his efforts to engage with the relevant bubbles during the tube trip to Fallopia. As I said before, *'Seed has no lead in his pencil.'* Not nearly enough to sustain his part in the overall coercing factor leading ultimately to Uterusa. The Pod is guilty of fraud. We rest our case." At this point, Judge Seiravo making another giant gesticulation with her hands - "more vitamin aid by the lorry load.

Recess for a six hour tea break before we sum up."

"Court will now resume," says the Usher. Judge Seiravo prepares to sum up. "Members of the Jury, all twelve honest Bubbles. There are two verdicts you must decide on regarding this case. On the one hand, the honesty and integrity of Pod. Did Pod deliberately set out to mislead the court over his intake of vitamin aid. If you decide he schemed about this matter - out for personal material gain rather than that of the universal soul. Then you must return a verdict of guilty.

If on the other hand, you feel Pod did everything possible to further the ensoulment of the womb chamber - including future conception and Universal development. If you feel there is overall evidence to support this - then a not guilty verdict is open to you. Concerning the case of Seed and his team of sperm Bubbles, I will give you Judicial advice. It would help if you considered the facts of the matter - did Seed have it in him, the energy and commitment to complete the repro mission.

If you think he did then a not guilty verdict for team Pod must be given. If on the other hand, you take the belief of the opposition that Seed was seedless - no lead in his pencil. Then the opposite conclusion must be arrived at."With this, the jury retired. However, after forty-five minutes, the verdict was ready. "Mr Foreman of the Jury." Says Judge Seiravo. "What is your verdict?" The Jury foreman stood up, a bespectacled Bubble with an envelope in his hand. "We the jury find the defendant Pod not guilty your Honor. In fact, we find the whole Pod team clear of any wrongdoing. In the case of Pod, we believe he acted out of noble and professional intentions. The charge of fraud not upheld in our collective viewpoint. In the instance of Seed, we did not find the evidence strong enough to convict. Seed did try to complete his task - there is no doubting his intentions or strength when it came down to the coercing of bubbles. The verdict is unanimous your Honor."

"You are free to go from this court," says the Judge. It's hard to explain the scene once the characters in this scenario go outside the courtroom. I will try for you, though. A mass of Bubbles are waiting for the defendants. They scream, shout, go mad. "Great job buddy, way to go Seed - you're the man Bubs." There is a group of Bubbles with posters - "change gonna come, man!" There were Bubbles with Bowlers - "Nice one chaps, put the bubble back in Britain." Some black bubbles looking like they are from the Caribbean. "Der soul gonna be born man - der soul comin." A group of gospel singing lady bubbles - *'Them seeds them seeds them dry seeds now hear the word of the lord.'*

Then there is a mass of Girlie type Bubbles. They are all screaming at the top of their voices. "Seed, Seed, Oh seed, Seed me. Marry me, Seed. Oh Pod, Pod, oh my Pod God." You could easily believe you were witnessing a boy band fanaticism. Or in their case a group of Popcorns. They were overnight stars, and here's why.

In the Judges chambers sits four people. Stamen the lawyer, Pod and Seed, plus Judge Seiravo. The Judge speaks: "Congratulations you did it. You won your case and the heart of the population. I'm awarding you an order of some magnitude plus all relevant costs. The inner body state awards you a mansion house with fifty rooms. Four kitchens, six bathroom en suites and a large garden area. The location, the temporal mindset of the outer Mother ship (state)."

It's at this point Pod starts asking questions. "If you dont mind your Honor where abouts is the location? The lady Judge looks squarely into Pods eyes before replying. "Near the left-sided ear, just above, firmly situated in the outer bodied Mother state. An extremely affluent part of the world - you and your team will see everything. She's a civil servant in this life but the karma repeats so our old friend the Universe will no doubt place her somewhere appropriate in the next."

Others chime in with support. "You should not have any trouble with it Pod," says Stamen. "You got a six hundred year karmic gap to get to grips with. And even then you may get a continued stay of execution, so to speak. Plenty of time to assimilate the outer body-mind of the Mother ship and adapt to the future karmic plan."

"The soul will make it this time Pod," says a more than relieved Seed. "Or should i say next. Yes, the next time we get into this position we should be able to shout a well-worn earthly phrase -

WE HAVE LIFT OFF HOUSTON."

CHAPTER 5 - THE HIGHER, MORE SIGNIFICANT LIFE

It's true, the spirit realms are more significant, more extensive, than the earth life. They have to be it's a bigger dimension in space and time. I will not bore you with mathematics. I leave it to experts, and there is enough of them out there. I want to cover a bit of the subject because it has essential value for us. I will explain soon.

First up, though, let us discuss some of the things that make up the higher, more comprehensive, more contemplative life that awaits us once we are ready. Once we leave the earth plane and ascend to the higher vibration, our viewpoint changes getting bigger, more significant; when souls reach a higher vibration, their minds grow in stature. In fact, souls leaving, studying their past. The viewpoint would be - that funny little life down there. Deffo.

Let me explain. When you exist on earth, it's like living in a box. This is putting it mildly. Some people would view it in a more serious light. It could be argued that we live in a life that resembles a prison. I believe it, but it's after we get beyond the material world that it becomes evident. Because our life here is earthy, material, and small in comparison with the higher dimension. It allows for a stunted, narrow, conception of things as opposed to the more elevated view. Even the best of us, the people with developed minds, even temperaments, can still fall foul of bigoted behaviour - full of prejudice. We cannot help it, part of living.

For instance, there is no such thing as racism in the spiritual life, it does not exist (Hallelujah). It cannot exist, no chance of it. In the higher concept, *all souls are bright - some are brighter than others.* But the fact is, they are all light-bodied souls - all one sheen for want of a better word.

Here on the earth plane, you cannot pretend it's never been an issue. In the past racism caused untold pain and suffering. And even, though, we are trying to move forward there are still pockets of resistance. We have not fully learned our lessons. But it can only happen here in the earth life nowhere else, only here in a matchbox type world that thrives on bigotry, ignorance, control, and copious amounts of greed.

Perhaps your mum and dad, passed, you never got to say goodbye, never said sorry for a misunderstanding, family issue. One of my clients even suggested to me; she feared that her mother in the spirit world hated her because she could not be present at her funeral. The problem rears its ugly head time and again.

So now I want to do something. I want to lay this blight of the mind to rest forever. I want to bury the misconception for good. Anyone who thinks in the way I have just described - stop. Stop now, this instant, wipe it out of memory. Because, I can tell you, the mindset, the thought pattern, the misplaced information in your head is so far offline. You might as well go and live on the moon. Its miles away and so is your thinking. People, it cannot happen and the quicker it is eliminated from the thought - the better. The reason? It's fundamental. The moment you leave the earth life and enter the higher version, your conception, viewpoint, change massively. You contemplate from a higher level, see the whole picture. You put yourself in another's place, see it from their point of view. It gives you objectivity. In the higher life, this form of viewpoint has a marked effect on how you evaluate. Plus, there is something else. You understand the gravity, perspective, of all issues. This mindset enables you to grade them, put them into the proper pecking order.

Nine out of ten times points we place great store upon in the material world are absolutely nothing in the life beyond. So, the argument that split a family up for twenty years in this world is basically, a puff of smoke in the next. It doesn't mean anything. It's not essential, hardly worth breaking sweat over. The more comprehensive viewpoint has no time for petty squabbles and jealous in-laws. Neither does it care that you got stuck in a traffic jam and missed your mum's funeral. Or, that you cheated on your partner and had an affair with six other people. I know it sounds terrible; I know it's not good to talk like this.

The point, though, being - in the higher life they don't care. It' of no consequence. Again, using an analogy. It's like looking into a wasp's nest. You haven't got a clue what they, the wasps, are doing. Milling around like idiots, they could be breaking every rule under the sun. Who would know it? Would you? Should men and women of our 21st-century disposition even dare to contemplate, watching paint dry will make time go quicker? In the next chapter, a short story. How a West Indian Lady stopped punishing herself over her Mother's death - gave herself a second lease of life.

LIFE IN A BOX - PUNISHMENT, THE STORY OF CARMEL JACKSON GRIFFITHS

Carmel Jackson Griffiths is a beautiful West Indian lady with two fantastic daughters and a great bloke of an English husband. She came to England in the early nineties when she was just a teenager. Carmel is massively proud of her Commonwealth roots, equally in love with Jamaican reggae and adores Solihull where they all live. Her finest hour when she met *Queen Elizabeth and Prince Phillip* in Birmingham City centre. A multicultural dream come true with one awful nightmare that continually haunts the mind.

Enter Gertrude Jackson, Carmel's deceased mum. It's a heart-rending story this and begins in Kingston, Jamaica in the mid to late 1970s. Carmel grew up in the Trench Town area of Kingston, living with mum Gertrude, dad Spencer. Residing with them, auntie Googie and Carmel's two sisters Prudence and Janine. It was far from a happy home. Dad Spencer always out of work, the family struggling to pay their way and survive.

Towards the late eighties things took a turn for the worse. Carmel's dad Spencer suddenly died. The cause of death unknown but it's generally agreed he went with heart failure. To England, they will now embark as a family. Carmel, her mum, auntie, and sisters all owned British passports. They will leave for the UK on the 7th June 1992, Carmel is sixteen years of age. The best-laid plans as they say - and yes, it went horribly wrong. On the day of departure, Carmel's sister Prudence fell ill with a stomach bug and could not make the trip. However, it's agreed that Auntie Googie and Carmel should go, leaving Prudence and Janine behind along with Carmel's mum Gertrude. She will stay with the two sisters and bring them over at a later date. A bit cockeyed if you want my opinion, but I've lived in a pokey little council flat for the last forty years with a cement bag over my head, so I'm clueless.

The final day, full of tears, Gertrude all hands and blub. "Ah love ma baby yer Mama comin for ya later sweetie." Auntie Googie is adding spice to the mini-drama. "Yeah, she be good, she gotta great schoolin to do - make her mommy proud. We comin back for you Gertie babe, yer gonna come here later. Yeah, you come wid us later." Tears, tears, and more blooming tears on top. But, you have to be in the heart of the Creole family lifestyle to appreciate the massive love and affection that goes down nine out of every ten seconds in a day. They get to Birmingham in England, Carmel, and her auntie Googie. It's at this point things start to change, not noticeable, hardly a sign. But the winds of time and circumstance beginning to stir.

Carmels progress in the UK is outstanding. She settles in brilliantly, Auntie Googie taking over as her mum while Gertrude is still in Jamaica. Over the next four years she is nothing short of staggering. She gets a degree in Social Welfare and lands a job with a local health authority - a managers role, Fab! But not everything comes right. The family back in Kingston. What of them? Ok, well, initially the plan was to come over within a year. It never materialized. The reason, not clear - not at this point. Carmel writes to her mum weekly, gets nothing back from Gertrude in the way of a reply. Gertrude, not brilliant at letter writing she leaves it to her two other daughters to correspond. Trouble is, they have very little to say and you get the feeling, family unity is on the drift.

Telephoning does not help either. Mobiles, still very much in the beginning stage so Carmel uses her home phone or a payphone in the street which costs a fortune. Still though, she cannot communicate. It gets worse, Carmel plans to catch a flight to Jamaica, only to discover she can't board the plane. She has contracted a rare syndrome, a fear of flying. Never apparent at the outset. But it's there now - can she ever meet her mum and sisters again?

As time passes the seemingly straightforward enough situation becomes more and more bizarre. It's near the end of the nineties, Carmel has taken to contacting her sisters by email. The two girls somehow managing a laptop between them. Trouble is they don't convey the messages to Gertrude. She is not aware that Carmel's been in touch. At this point, I want to explain a few things.

The two sisters have changed dramatically. They do not like Carmel, nor do they try to hide the fact. They resent not coming to the UK but will never think of doing anything about it. They are deteriorating - it's beginning to show. Both girls piling on calories. I think it is fair to say they are grossly overweight. Yet, all they do is lounge about and eat until sick. Yes sick, deffo. The Mother shakes her head in despair. They were so cute when young, now look!

The whole thing getting unreal, resembling a panto play - *Cinderella and the two podgy Gannets*. Well, they're hardly tiny fairies anymore - all they do is pig out, bitch incessantly. Throughout, Gertrude not aware of the sniping. She's sad Carmel is not in touch, or so she believes. No anger here, just desperation to see her little girl again. Gertrude loves Carmel deeply; she always makes excuses for her.

Time moves forward, we enter a grey period. I have my suspicions mum unwell, taken to her bed. Two podgy birds make hay while the sun shines. In between sending fraudulent emails to Carmel regarding Gertrude's wellbeing, they continue to gorge. An oversized, creole type, meatball downed in one take - off the plate in two ferocious gulps. If this was a match between Herring gulls and women. The two females win - no sweat.

Carmel in the meantime has suspicions. She's not spoken to mum properly for some time and is worried. Then one Sunday morning totally out of the blue an email message, Gertrude is gone! Passed away in her sleep. Tears all day and night and far into the future and to make it worse, Carmel cannot attend the funeral. She will be ill with the flight, and it's agreed that auntie Googie will go to the sad event. The real damage takes time but creeps up on Carmel like fog - a fog of guilt and shame.

"She hates me Auntie, 'Mama' hates me. I wasn't there for her. Didn't even get to her funeral." "No, baba no. Yer Mama ain't never been like it. She got love for you child. You were der favourite girl. Always, yeah, always." It's not enough though, Not nearly enough to ease Carmel's, broken heart. Depression creeps in slowly, poisonously, degrading to watch. She ages through the anxiety of it all. Plus, the sisters have stopped all communique. The blame game for something the poor girl has no clue over. Carmel's career suffers. She is granted extended sick leave by the local authority she works for - but it won't last long. She has to sort her life out quick before things get out of hand.

Then a miracle happens. Carmel visits a psychic lady who does mediumship in Dudley, West Midlands. **Mother Meason,** or **Lynne** as she is better known. Lynne picks Gertrude up immediately. Describes her to Carmel, then proceeds to tell her things. "Your mum is crying, loads of tears in her eyes. She's hurting, but it's not quite what you think. Mum is sad because you doubt her love. You think she's deserted you, doesn't love you anymore - I'm being told that's cobblers."

Carmel looks shocked. This girl is banging it out, right on the nose. Lynne continues. "Your Mothers got massive feelings for you; they can never die. Have faith in her and you. She's telling me one more thing. Soon you will get evidence, will know in your heart exactly how she's feeling. God bless your dear mum; she is a wonderful soul." Carmel has tears in the eyes as she leaves. The psychic Lynne, quite a girl and she was nail on with a lot of stuff. But there are still doubts, the bit about evidence. She can't grasp the bit where she spoke of evidence. What evidence? No fretting dear lady -

YOU ARE ABOUT TO FIND OUT

A few weeks go by. In this period, some subtle and unexplained twists. Carmel notices a lot of flickering lights in the room. Clocks going wrong for no apparent reason. One particular day she witnessed a small alarm clock turn around on its own - as if guided by a pair of invisible hands. Weird things of late. Then, one mind-blowing night something happens, that will change the course of Carmel's life forever. She has a vivid, strange, mysterious dream. When I say vivid, I mean as clear as crystal. Everything seemingly going down right in front of her eyes. It's a bit complex this but will do my best to explain.

The scene, a late 1960s disco type club in upmarket Kingston, Jamaica. There are swish dudes, and fabulous mini-skirted girls dancing. Playing in the background pure Jamaican Reggae beat and Ska soul. The place, alive, with cool action and sophisticated nostalgia. Carmel finds herself right in the centre, sitting at a table sipping Cuba Libre, well iced. On the dance floor swaying to the infectious rhythm, a willowy, tall, good looking girl with a super figure. She's got lovely thick West Indian hair down to her shoulders. Looks slightly like a young *Diana Ross* when she was just starting out with *Motown*.

Carmel is drawn to this lady. In fact, can't take her eyes off her. Also, she feels she knows her but cannot think where they met. The lady smiles, waves at her while she sits at the table with her drink. The club is heating up, people pouring in. Behind the chatter and excitement, the infectious tones of :

Prince Simeon Mekka and the Ram Band - Banu Como Luna (Blood Moon).

'You think you doing good, i think you doing fine
The akka coming quick the sugar all be mine
Banu Como, the possibility there, she know it there
Banu Como, she know it right, it's always right
The nanny goat tight, blood moon in sight
Yeeeeeah, Yeeeeeeahh'
Prince Simeon Mekka - 1969 Tomb records

The scene feels like it goes on forever. Carmel is sipping her drink while watching the swishy girl dancing away, a bevy of male attention hovering. Then, in a jiffy, like dreams tend to do - the whole scene changes. Suddenly, as if by magic, the dancing queen was next to her. Looking right into her eyes, smiling beautifully, she speaks. "How are you, baby, how have you been?" Carmel is shocked. The woman's tone suggesting more than just a casual salutation. She talked like she knew. Still smiling, the lady takes her hand and kisses it. "Look at me, Carmel, study me deeply. Don't you know me?" Carmel looks and keeps looking, and then it dawns.

'OH MY GOD,' the penny dropping in a flash. It is her Mother; Carmel is looking at her Mother. But how? How could this be, so young and beautiful, and the speech so eloquent? The Creole lingo of yesteryear - gone. In its place polished dialogue. Hardly surprising. After all, it's a higher vibration - a more refined ego. Carmel has tears in her eyes. She holds on tight to her Mothers hand. " 'Mama, oh Mama,' it's you, it's really you. But how? You look so young, speak so graceful." "You did it for me, Carmel. You made me baby" Carmel is gobsmacked but gets the reply in. "How, though?" The re-refined Gertrude smiles. "Your love for me honey, your deep emotional feelings spread over time. Healed me and rejuvenated me when I went over. Plus, I could see from higher ground."

Carmel looks dazed. "What do you mean higher ground?" "The whole picture Carmel. I saw the whole thing from start to finish - your lovely feelings for me right from being a little girl. Oh bless. I know, things got in the way, time, circumstances. They always do. You just forgive and move on; it's no big deal. Life is no big deal, baby. It's all so fast, so very fast. Something I learned when I got here."

Carmel can feel tears. "Mama, what shall I do." Gertrude strokes her face gently. "Nothing dear child, nothing drastic. Lead your life and give yourself credit. You done fantastic; we are all proud of you in the higher world. Go easy and remember. Your Mama loves you forever nothing in the Universe can change or destroy. I'm here for you, watching you, protecting you, waiting for you. Oh, and be nice to your sisters. They don't mean anything. They are just confused, need a bit of enlightenment coupled with a fish and water diet." She smiles longingly, and with this, the scene fades, Carmel wakes up. She now feels so good - kind of like weight taken off the shoulders. The dream was life-like, a book of pictures. Every scene an informative story. Already the depression is fading. If there are any doubts over Carmel's psychic visions, they are about to be eliminated. Fixing a coffee for herself, she turns on the radio...

'I see you in the night the poppin give a feel
Nanny goat run she gotta do der deal
Banu Como, the sensible way, the moon on ice
the possibility there, she know it there
Banu Como, she know it right, it's always right
The sweet nanny goat tight, blood moon in sight,
Yeeeeeah, Yeeeeeeahh'
Prince Simeon Mekka - 1969 Tomb records

Before seeking recourse to a box of Kleenex, I pose a question. What do we deduce from Carmel's story? Well, one thing is obvious. The moment you leave earth life and gravitate to a higher vibration, all narrow mindedness, and petty ways of seeing things disappear. You contemplate the whole rather than a just part of it. Carmel's mother Gertrude was a testament to this. She passed and saw the whole picture. Subsequently, saw things exactly as they are, able to place them in perspective. Carmel was distraught because she believed her mum hated her for not attending the funeral. Gertrude didn't even think of it.

  Whether she attended her funeral or not was of little importance. Why? Because she saw the entire viewpoint, not just a segment. The whole picture is unanimous in supporting Gertrude's feeling for Carmel - she loves her dearly. Going to a funeral, baptism, birthday party or wedding will not change anything. Like Gertrude said: it's no big deal, no one in the higher life is bothered. All the worry, pain, and anxiety lie here in earth life.

Think deep on this, resonate over time. The love you cultivate while you are here on the material plane stays regardless. If you think in a similar way to Carmel - stop! Stop it now and never dwell on it again. If you do, then you're not fair to yourself or those who have passed. You are hurting you and them unnecessarily. Take some mind fresh and ponder.

CHAPTER 6 - BIRTH OF THE SOUL

What does a soul look like when you first see it? In the beginning stages of ascending, it is small. If you could see it emerging from the body, it resembles a small sphere with a bit of a wispy tail. It's kind of like a comet. People have seen the soul, captured it on film. The small, spherical, ball of energy develops quickly in the spirit world. Grows fast, beyond itself in comparison with how a young child would on the earth plane. In some ways, though, there is a comparison with how babies are born here and how souls ascend to a higher life.

When a child is born, people gather. Midwife, Nurse, family, friends, and helpers. Even husbands and boyfriends. When souls are ready to leave under normal circumstances, deceased relatives, friends, gather to receive them. A child is born in this life, and the midwife snips the umbilical cord that connected baby to Mother in the womb. A soul ascends to the higher consciousness, the silver cord connecting body and soul breaks. We come into the earth life, our Mother sustains us, nourishes, and cares for us while young and beyond. But we have another Mother - *Planet Earth*. Mother Earth continues our development, prepares us for the higher life. In the final analysis, she lets her children go. Releases them, allows them to ascend to the higher vibration where the soul continues its journey.

A young aspiring soul grows in the higher world, similar to how we do here but quicker. It's not the same as being a baby in this life. In the sense of, the fragility of being young, sleeping all day, can't remember much. In the spiritual life, souls go over, remembering all they accomplished on the earth plane. The soul develops in the higher consciousness - so what does it look like form-wise, resemble? Similar to this life but more enhanced, brighter, more defined. When you ascend to the spirit world, you are still you. The Universe will not allow you to become a ten-headed monster. You are you, and you look like you. Because, though, it is a higher life, there are subtle changes.

Let us study the changes. When you are born to this life, you rely on your parent's genetic makeup to give you a fair deal if you are a nice-looking child with a healthy disposition, brill. If you have a few quirks physically, not so good. You cannot do much about it either way regarding how you look except possibly have corrective surgery later on. The life here is not an even playing field and is subject to vicious elements of unrequited fate, circumstances.

In earth life, you can be physically beautiful or not, so if you are gorgeous doors open. People like you, lust over you, think you're the most fantastic person that ever lived. And guess what? You probably are - so we don't knock it. But if you are unfortunate enough to be born the opposite, then it's not so promising. Doors close, people not that interested, and I doubt they will squirm around you.

There are exceptions to the rule of course - one of them is wealth. If you are downright innocuous but massively wealthy, people make excuses. The life here, shallow, and misleading. A trap into which we all fall - no exceptions. The tragedy of living an earth life is that you can be the kindest hearted person in the Universe - but the masses judge you on how you look and what you have in the bank.

In the higher life, it is entirely different. For instance, you cannot be any other than good looking when you're in a higher vibration - no chance of the opposite. Souls are fundamentally beautiful. How? Several reasons. When you leave the earth plane and evolve into a higher existence, you drop your physical body. Your body goes, and your soul starts to develop on its own. The body is matter the soul is energy. Matter deteriorates and gets ugly. Energy never ages and self rejuvenates.

Both have a form that can be seen by others sharing the same dimension. Souls in higher life are pure energy as opposed to flesh and bone, so there is no ageing process. Your body, as such, in a higher vibration, is light (Merkaba). Here it is dense. Because the light body soul of the spirit world consists of energy, it remains consistent, bright, self-rejuvenating and powerful. There are no quirks, bumps, or distortions like you see here.

The higher life energy stays at one power level allowing you to assume the form of an angel as opposed to a human being. So it does not matter what you looked like on the earth. In the higher life, you become regular, consistent, angelic in appearance - or at least to a greater degree.

All SOULS ARE DIVINE - SOME MORE SO

Beauty, as they say, is in the eye of the beholder. You hear this quoted by a lot of people and it's true. But you can bet your life, whatever preference we have for those we fancy; there has to be something physically engaging about them to move our emotions. In other words, lovely hair, beautiful eyes, high cheekbones, or an adorable figure. Couple this to the way they smile or look at us. It all adds to our perception of beauty.

The trouble is, in lots of cases, the beauty fails to match the personality. Some of the most gorgeous people in the world are the nastiest. Or, have ego's so bloated - you cannot live with them. Of course, when you look at the person, your hard-pressed to see it. Butter can't melt in some people's mouths. Yet, they're as ghastly as hell. It's a fact, and we all know it.

In the higher life, this problem does not exist. As already mentioned, in the higher vibration, we cannot be any other than good looking. Even *Quasimodo* would look good after ascending to the higher realms. The bumps, the boils, the facial misdemeanours, all disappear when on ascending. They cannot exist in the higher life. But beauty in the spirit world is dual dimensional. Not just about good looks and nothing else.

In the earth life, beauty exists in the eyes. You look at a beautiful girl; you do not know what she is like as a person. You cannot see her mind. In the higher life, when you look at someone, you not only see them form-wise - you understand their nature. In the sense of, see the kind of person they are how they feel about others. The concept of beauty in the higher world takes on another dimension - a dual role. The general perception of beauty, good looks, is not just the way you appear to others. It becomes how you think and feel. The mindset, an essential part of determining your **WOW** factor! Beauty, good looks, sex appeal, whatever you want to call it - becomes dual dimensional. So, if you were a fantastic looking person on the earth plane but could not give two hoots about people and their feelings, then, when you pass over to the spirit world - you lose the edge. You still look good form wise. But you lack, the personality, not there, does not match the looks. You are missing a vital ingredient, and it has consequences. You are divine but not as divine as some. Therefore, the edge you had in this life takes a back-seat role. Others get the adoration - you drop down the pecking order.

In a strange way it's like looking at two perfect cakes. They both look fantastic - Mmmm. The difference, one tastes divine, the other bland. They both look good but only one is special inside.

SHAPESHIFTING

In the higher life, you look good. I have said this enough times to make you realize, the truth of it. There is, though, more to this than recognized or spoke about in earnest. In the spirit world, you *shapeshift*, enhance yourself. What does it mean? Well, in this life if we are not satisfied with aspects of our features. We do something about it. Pay a cosmetic surgeon to put us right. Make us beautiful so we can face the world in a more positive light. Trouble is it costs a fortune. In the higher life, you get similar treatments, except, you create them yourself - you *shapeshift*.

Shapeshifting depends on fifth-dimensional thinking. This line of thought is where you think something, and it happens. A form of advanced visualization, you see it in your mind, go ahead and manifest it. Shapeshifting is the ability to create subtle, finesse like, enhancements to your soul energy body, implementing them at will.

When you shapeshift, you see something in your mind's eye, and it manifests. So if you're looking for a little depth to your features, you think it, see it, fit it into your facial expression. The way you visualize it in your mind - hey presto, it appears like a subtle makeover. It's a form of fifth-dimensional thinking because you think, see, and implement. All achieved through the power of thought and mind concentration. What is more you make it happen in seconds.

We can shapeshift on the earth plane. But it's crude when you compare it to the natural, inherent, abilities we have at our disposal in the higher life. Shapeshifting in the spirit world is a natural trait you use at will. It allows for subtle enhancements and highlights. But it will not change you into someone else. It's not going to make you look like *Elvis Presley* if you get my drift. Shapeshifting, gives us that little bit of style, highlighting that we can't always produce. Think of the best day of your life when you looked in the mirror and thought, yes that's it, the look I want. When you shapeshift, you only have to believe it - you get it at will.

JOBS IN THE HIGHER LIFE

Is there work once you pass over? In short, yes, but not like here. On planet Earth, we create, manufacture, service, care, etc., to survive. In the higher life, you do not have to be industrious unless you want to be. I give reasons to support this later. The whole ball game changes when you enter the spirit world. The life, euphoric as opposed to stressful. Time flows, no beginnings, no endings. You do not need to clock watch. In the higher consciousness, there are no pressing obligations to meet like there are here.

And, one of the most significant factors - you do not need money. But, say, for instance, you wanted money. Well, you create it from your thoughts. Over the years, during thousands of *I Ching readings* - which is what I do. I have formulated through a series of complicated channellings, information that I want to share with you. I stress, the information did not appear overnight. It took a little while to make sense of it, get it in order.

There are three categories relating to work-life, industry, career, in the higher world. I list them for you.

1 - CARE AND THERAPY FOR THE SOUL

2 - MANIFESTING A WORK LIFE REALITY

3 - SOULS, SUM TOTAL OF THEIR EXISTENCE

Number one, care and soul therapy. When soul's pass over to the spiritual life, they bring their minds, not their bodies. The body, or remains, cremated, or buried on the earth plane. We all know this to be true. In a lot of cases, the minds of souls are damaged, need repairing. Living on the earth plane takes a toll. Souls get brainwashed, misled, stressed out to the point where they experience a breakdown and mental damage. All of these problems need to be taken care of in the spiritual life. So one of the main areas of work for a soul is mental and emotional therapy. The treatments, cures, are of a high level and only experts in the field of medicine, mental health, nursing, would be expected to undertake the task. This descriptive situation is not so. It's an open playing field regarding who gets involved. A lot of souls who worked on the earth plane in hospitals, clinics, doctors surgeries do well here. But ordinary people who did no more than care about their fellow men and women also thrive. Qualifications concerning medicine do not count because there is no physical body. But if you loved your neighbour, tried to help rather than hinder, gave a little here and there. You can go right to the very top.

So the little old lady who had no experience of the medical profession but gave ten cups of tea to several workers digging her road. She can be right up there. Right at the top of the tree because she gave of herself willingly, had the mindset to understand what people wanted at that moment in time. Souls who work in the therapy and care area will never be short of work. Eighty per cent of all the souls who ascend need help. The damage when you come to earth life is massive.

Another area is anger management. Lots of souls go over with this problem. They are angry at the way things worked out for them or didn't. One main cause of anger on the earth plane is the injustices of society. People see things like murderers set free after only serving a few years in prison. People who make millions of pounds drug dealing while they struggle to pay their rent.

People cross over in an angry state; they need therapy, guidance, periods of reflection under supervision to assimilate why things happen in the way they do here. Millions of souls will gravitate to a higher life of care and therapy towards other souls, which begs the question. Do you want to work in a higher consciousness? *Hey Baby, you got the job.*

MANIFESTING A WORK LIFE REALITY

Some souls do not want to work. In terms of they do not want to go down the therapy, recuperation route. It's a free choice, and if you don't want to get involved, you do not have to. When you aspire to a higher life, you automatically manifest whatever you want. It's all part of the fifth-dimensional thought process where you think of something you want to happen, or an object you want to create - it happens. Whatever you wish, believe for, there in front of you. You manifest it in your life.

This progressive thinking opens a wealth of opportunities for souls to get involved. You create personal reality. We saw a bit of this in the story of Bert Brown earlier. You create a virtual reality lifestyle for whatever you want. Some souls do it brilliantly; others, struggle with it. In a way, it is like *Simon Cowell's X Factor tv show.* People who want to be TV stars in regard to singing, dancing, etc. Wannabees they may be, some though, talented, and professional in their own right. You are manifesting your reality in higher life in a similar way. Some souls brilliant at it others not.

Higher souls help you create your dreams and available to coach you. Similar to this world. People ready to instruct and bring you on in whatever field you aspire to. Manifestation in the higher realms is a mind-blowing experience to look forward to. Once you realize what it is, how it works, it pales into insignificance anything your ego could produce here. For instance, if you were a pop star, who passed into the higher life, started telling everyone how much money you made, how many women you spent the night with. Other souls laugh at you. They laugh because it is nothing special. We can all do it …it's easy.

SOULS - SUM TOTAL OF THEIR EXISTENCE

One of the main reasons you do not have to work in a higher life unless you want to - *you have already done it, completed the job.* The Universe is a clever animal. All the time you existed on the earth plane you were working. I don't mean working for a business, your day job, etc., etc. I do not mean any of these things. I'm saying, you were working for the Universe every day of your earthly life. Perhaps you didn't know it, did not consider. It's true though; the Universe is your boss while you are here and as such supports you.

In a way, every one of us is like a piece of software in a computer program, gathering information, storing it in our memory banks. We do it every day of our lives from the minute we are born. Every person no matter who they are, a hive of knowledge and learning. An advanced level of energy source for higher intelligence to analyse and solve. A form of debriefing, constantly analyzed is what takes place. We as human beings like to imagine we have free choice. I don't think there is any.

When we come to the earth plane, we store experiences in mind and memory. Every little facet of what we feel, do, saved as part of our development. The time spent here doing all the mundane things that earth existence offers. Nothing wasted, nothing extra added, just pure actions and the experience gained through those actions.

Which goes to prove one thing. No person how big or small they consider themselves leaves this earth life without some form of contribution. You may believe that you are the most insignificant person that ever lived. But, in the eyes of the Universe, you just made a marvellous play. You lived and died. In this time you did a multitude of things, some considered good, others not so good. Also, there was a time in life where you might have experienced indifference. A bag load of it! But that's the nature of the world we exist in - boring as hell. or the very though of it.

The thing is though, you did it, made it, lived through the whole *god darned spectacle called life.* Give yourself a break. You came, completed, got the tee-shirt -

YOU ARE SPECIAL

And because you got through it your experiences, recorded, logged, stored within you for posterity.

Saved for a day in the universal future when they will be analysed and acted upon, put into play. In a way, leaving this life to ascend is like one giant debriefing exercise. In the sense of, once we reach the higher realms, we become data, input, food for higher intelligence. The Universe, one giant mouth through which we all disappear. Nothing added, taken away. Everything of use great or small.

CHAPTER 7 - MORE FIFTH DIMENSIONAL THINKING AND THE HIGHER LIFE

You think, and it is. You see circumstances in your mind, they happen. Imagine on a day to day basis the amount of time saved. The higher life is instant, the lower world, slow, tedious, and tiring. Take getting up in the morning. Look what you go through in this life to keep looking good. You wash, hair, teeth, eyes, nails, and ears. Think about it. The time spent on a tedious but essential duty. Day after day after day.

Compare it to what happens in a parallel scenario in the spirit world. In the higher life, you do not have to rise early in the morning. Simply because there is no beginning or ending regarding time, but consider this, if you did sleep and arose from it, wanted to groom yourself. How long would it take - the answer: instant makeover. In a split second, you look your best. In a sense, your skin glows, your eyes are bright, hair perfectly styled. The form is good.

Perhaps you want to go somewhere, a journey. In this life, you are subjected to a serious amount of planning, even if it's only a bus ride. You must know what and which bus to catch. If it's a train, you have to be sure of timetables, connections, and the purchase of tickets. All time consuming and likely to put you under a certain amount of coercion and worry. In the higher life, you travel by transforming your soul energy body into a vehicle of transport. Imagine it, from A to B at the speed of thought.

The higher life, a replica of this life but more to it in terms of content, lifestyle, viewpoint, in the higher world people still build houses. They do not purchase the property or run around doing a mission impossible - trying to get a mortgage. They design and build from their mind. The places, fantastic in terms of shape, colour schemes, and dimensions, designed by the mind, built from imagination. The ability to manifest one sizeable chunk of higher world reality and create it from your mindset. Total cost = **NOTHING.** Certainly in terms of money which in the higher life does not exist. I say, does not exist. Let's put it this way, is not needed. When you do anything in the higher world - it's already paid. You did it when you were here on the earth plane.

When you need a house in this life, you seek recourse to your bank and hope for a little generosity. In a sense, you are asking to go to a mental institute. More realism to be had there than favours from a bank manager. But in the spirit world you relax, the total of your earthy existence has more than covered the desire for comfort and lifestyle. The Universe is a great boss to work for and will pay far more than any earthbound organization. The higher the mindset, the more social empathy shown to a stranger, the ability to separate money from ethics. Traits that promise a millionaire lifestyle in a higher life if you can pull it off.

What does higher life resemble in terms of flower and fauna? There are flowers and trees and vast expanses of greenery such as fields, lawns, and parkland. In the higher vibration, the flowers are remarkable. For instance, the colours mind-blowing. There are subtle shades never experienced while on the earth plane. Blooms, massive in appearance and because the vibration is higher, plant life develops a language. This language thing is not to say they will talk to each other like human beings do. There will be though, a universal plant lingo that to the naked ear might appear as a soft hushed toned down whistling sound. Not shrill like here on earth. More a subtle shade of tone, easy on the ear, therapeutic to the mind. The sky in a higher life is much the same as here a deep radiant blue. But unlike planet earth, you never get grey leaden days full of rain and wind.

The weather in spiritual life is temperate not to hot and not cold. More a pleasantly even temperature with a Warm bright feel as opposed to the dark and chill atmosphere. The higher vibration is euphoric. You never feel put out by diversity of climate as experienced on the earth world.

Think about this scenario in detail. If we on the Earth plane had constant sunny weather. Not to hot, just perfect, how would we feel? You would witness more laughing than crying.

THE HIGHER LIFE FAST - INCREDIBLY FAST

The higher world is fast - fifty thousand times faster than life here, an excellent analogy to describe it. In the life here we get used to things such as fibre optics and super broadband, and for us, on planet earth, they are mega quick. But in the higher dimension, this kind of thing is the stuff of dinosaurs. As old as the hills, junkyard garbage. One of the reasons you cannot see divine light-bodied forces is because of the dimensional speed in which they operate. So fast you blink and there gone, disappeared to the naked eye. The talk so quick you can never hear it.

Though, sometimes, if you're receptive in a spiritual sense. You may see a symbol, a string of images, resonating in the mind but not sure what to make of it, what it means. In a lot of cases, spirits visit people just before they get off to sleep. The mind, soul, flickering to a low vibrational ebb and allowing higher-dimensional souls the chance to make contact. The language of the higher dimensions is symbolic as opposed to being verbal. They contact through image based telethapy rather than dialogue. This is one of the reasons mediums and Psychics have their uses - they convey the symbols, turn the picture language into something tangible so we can understand it through the spoken word.

Dreams are another media from which the higher souls operate, so vivid it's like you are there in person. If you could see with the naked earth eye into the earth atmosphere, you would be amazed at the amount of higher life energies going about their day. The sky filled with individual light-bodied souls. This situation, though, the painful enigma. Until we gravitate to the higher life, we can never truly understand the mind-blowing world that awaits us. It will come, and when it does, we will embrace it effortlessly.

CHAPTER 8 - WHY DO SOULS COME HERE - BEGINNINGS

Not an easy question to answer, so many theories. Nobody knows. The author of this book doesn't know. I can only give the results of my incessant channelings over the years. The approach put forward based upon them and not dissimilar to those documented by the late *Edgar Cayce* (sleeping prophet). This similar viewpoint evident, and I run the risk of accusations relating to plagiarism. If so, then no worries on my part. The American psychic *Edgar Cayce,* in my opinion, brilliant, gifted, someone I revere. If my name ever gets mentioned with his - good or bad, then I shall feel wonderfully privileged.

Souls in higher life have no material body. Indeed they have no material form like they did when existing on the earth plane. As already mentioned in earlier chapters, they exist as higher soul energies. Actions replaced by thoughts - spoken language replaced by symbolism.

One thing, though, does not change - the ego. Souls who have gravitated to the higher realms still have an ego. They have it and express it much as possible. But, here lies the dilemma as much as the spiritual world is a brilliant, safe, and euphoric dimension. It's hardly the ideal place for an over-ambitious ego, not a centre stage for universal adoration.

Of course, we know souls can manifest in higher life, create their reality. A place where they do all things and become all things, it's not quite the same, though - it's not solid. Being in a physical form has got its plus points. The earth life has benefits and being in a body one of them. When you're in a tangible format, you make physical actions, wordy statements. You stand up, shout, and people look at you. You express yourself through your ego, and people take note. They may not necessarily like what they see or hear. But feelings expressed, the overblown ego standing up, making a spectacle, getting recognised. In a sense, being on the earth plane and showing the ego is like being on television - live on air.

Plus, you get sexual satisfaction. You give vent to your bodily desires and feelings through sexual contact. Express your ego through physical higher life fantasies, the sheer delight of being with your wife, husband, and partner. In a way, you can also achieve this or something similar in the higher vibration. But there is nothing like being physical in a physical world - like everything else in the universal plan, got its attributes. Nothing without purpose or planning, nothing wasted past and present.

Souls came to this life aeons back when the planet, newly formed, and the ecosystem was getting into its stride. They came as energised thought forms and looked down upon the earth, gravitated to the planet life without getting involved. There was a bag load of them - thought forms with neither body nor purpose. Free to roam as they wished upon the material planes of existence without getting caught up in any of the crude life forms developing at the time. It went on for a while, probably a few million years and then something unusual happened.

One or a few thought forms (souls) entered the flesh. They did it on the spur of the moment with no particular reason other than a mischievous free choice. Something that gets human beings into trouble many times in the future. Souls entered matter at will and left it similarly. They pushed themselves in, pushed out. As I say, the original part probably some dare or investigative, curiosity, process.

Once one had accomplished it, a few more gave it a go. Similar to dipping toes into freezing surf on a shoreline. What's it like how does it feel? You've never been there, so it becomes a bit of an obsession to take a chance. Like all experiments, though, something invariably goes astray - no exceptions to the rule.

When I say souls entered matter, I am talking about the crude forms of life that existed on the earth a few million years back. In a sense, primaeval man. The first dare of entering flesh, experiencing the feeling of being humanoid. A crude form of pleasure-seeking, a thrill.

Plus, It gave purpose to the soul minded ego - let it off the leash. How was it accomplished, though? How did they get in? It was a violation of a lower being by a higher form of intelligence. This enforced behaviour is not allowed by universal law, but it did not deter the souls from doing it. Like I say, at first, it was a game, a dare. They entered matter and got out at will, kept it going like this for a more extended period than they should have.

Then, and more likely in a sudden sense than any other, the inevitable happened. Souls became trapped could not get out of the flesh body they had taken over. They got caught in the material by their interfering ego. The exciting game of entering flesh, experiencing the pleasures of life and lust turning the tables on them, condemning them to a life and death process on an alien planet.

In a sense, millions of miles from home. Forced participation in the karmic comings and goings of something and someone never meant to be. Once souls found themselves trapped, it was inevitable to form a rescue program to offset what had gone wrong. So, the cry goes up in the higher realms - volunteers needed. A billion souls respond. But the thing is, there is no quick rescue.

Once involved, tied to something or someone you become part of the karmic process and it never ends. It's a lesson Politicians and Prime Ministers more than anyone should heed. Think twice before going into a foreign land with a mindset to take it over. The short term profits of being victorious, looking saint-like, pale into insignificance when you realise what awaits in the long run. Binding yourself and others to the Nation violated, imprinting your philosophy and mindset upon their ego - cloning them, binding you to their karma. Paying for something that was never a part of your karmic plan until you made it so, condemning not only you but others who come after. Picking up the tab and paying off a never-ending debt ultimately left by you and your over bloated ego!

Souls, trapped, and even though a billion force rescue plan put into operation, there is no way out. As time passes, they adjust to the physical forms they violated to create a never-ending struggle - primitive force versus divine energy. Constant comings and goings of the karmic life cycle, each new incarnation a little more comfortable than the last - but still a mountain to climb. No way of getting off the planet for good. What started as a mild experiment to stimulate an innocent ego, now an ongoing nightmare of power struggle. And yet, separate the two, the soul energy from the physical. You will always find the soul in its entirety still as pure as it was in the very beginning. The essential nature of men and women a divine one. How, though, will it all end? How will we, as pure souls, rid ourselves from this awful experiment gone wrong?

The answer: we won't. We can't. Nothing will happen if left to our own devices - we need universal help. The Universe will ultimately rescue us. As already discussed, a shift will happen. It's all we need, a widespread change in consciousness. Even a slight dimensional rise in frequency can solve our problem. Separate us from the mass, materialistic, mindset that stops our progression as a race. But when will this happen? No one has a clue on planet earth.

Only the Universe knows the exact moment of timing. When it happens, finally goes ahead, we will be aware of it. As a race, we will feel it in an instant - in the twinkling of an eye!

CHAPTER 9 - EMPTY SOULS
THE DARK ZONE

As much as there are light-bodied souls who come and go in life, there are also negative, troubled, ones who hang about. These souls do not pass over and stay around the earth plane for whatever reason suits them. It's a fact; not every soul has a clear cut plan to ascend the higher regions of the Universe. Some souls on the point of death can be as negative as the thought of hell, and instead of rising to the spiritual life or gravitating to loved ones left behind, they find a suitable spot to dwell while they wait for a future incarnation. Sometimes, the place of dwelling can be another person's body and mind.

Let me explain further. We know from reading not just this book but others of similar profile - all souls in the Universe have free choice. All part and parcel of universal law. As already covered ninety per cent of souls who come and go will either ascend to the higher vibration or gravitate to loved ones left behind. They, then, move over a little later on a singular basis or collectively.

Some people die lonely deaths. This statement an accepted truth that if thought about long enough can make us feel uneasy and sad. But you have to face it. It happens every day of the week. People die alone, and it's not just the loneliness that causes problems. A lot of times the death occurs in dire and painful circumstances. Some people have no one in the world to care about them. No relatives, dependants. There are times when people become invisible - no one knows they are there. No blame attached either, as already discussed, life here is singular as opposed to group orientated. You cannot always look out for people - we all have our daily grind.

When a person who is lonely and unloved in life dies - a multitude of souls will gather and do everything they can to make things right. The chances are that in the higher consciousness, there will be souls who know the newly deceased and will gather anyway. So no one dies and goes to the higher realms desolate - it's not possible. But here is the problem, some people do not want to leave. They do not want to quit life, and they are not bothered who loves them or doesn't, both here or in the higher world. They do not give a fig, either way; they want to dwell, stay, find another person to join. In a sense, kill time. It's not all about being lonely either. Some people do things in life, leaving them with eternal shame or a multitude of fear.

In some cases, a crime, an evil, a dark secret that cannot come out. So fear traps them. The fear of retribution, punishment. The shame of being exposed. This fright is why some souls, once they leave the earth plane, cannot gravitate to the light - exposure on a big scale. If they did pass over, there would be a massive surprise for them - no one judges you. Only you know where you have been and what you have done. So only you evaluate your actions regarding right or wrong. There is no punishment.

The people I have described who stay on the earth plane are not necessarily bad or evil. As already stated, all souls are pure. It's when they come here; they get tainted when they come to earth life. The type of soul who roams the earth plane without trying to ascend is usually heavy into drugs or hiding evils that have not come to life. The chronic drug addict sometimes will not leave because of the addiction. The higher world gravity will not pull them over - they desire the cravings, thrills, fantasies of the flesh. So they stay, gravitate to the earth plane, hover, usually somewhere near to where they lived and eventually died.

Evil criminals are also similar, will not dare ascend to the light for fear of being punished, which goes to show that all souls understand the seriousness of what they did or didn't do right in the life. It's just that in a sense they could not help themselves. They had to succumb to whatever lusts and pleasures they felt were essential at the time. I call these souls - Empty Souls because this is what they are empty, void of all feelings regarding accomplishing anything. They drift aimlessly in search of shelter. Yes, shelter. Somewhere they can be safe, rehoused in a body. In a sense, continue their life in another persons skin!

Empty souls nine times out of ten do not pose a problem in life, but there are exceptions to the rule. There are times where they will force entry and take over another person's mind. Allow me to explain. Ninety-nine per cent of the time you are safe from being invaded by empty souls (drifting souls). It will not happen, and by universal law, it is not allowed to happen. But there can be breaches to any laws. An empty soul can only violate another soul if:

A - <u>They force the entry and</u>..

B- <u>The conditions enabling forced entry are suitable</u>

When I say forced entry, I mean that they enter your body and to a degree, your mind - forcibly, without expressed permission. Under normal circumstances, it can never happen, so I don't want anyone to start having panic attacks or die of fear. But like i say there are exceptions to the rule and we will deal with them one by one.

There are three main areas, conditions, where empty souls will violate another souls body and mind.

1 - the use of an Ouija board.

If you use an Ouija board then, in my opinion, you are playing with death. They are as dangerous as hell (or the thought of it), and you must avoid them at all costs. When performing on an Ouija board, you try contacting spirits of those who have gone over to the other side. Nine out of ten times you can get away with a harmless séance type experience with your friends, nothing happens to you.

But you play the board one night, and something unsavoury is lurking in the regions above or around you - it can be fatal, In terms of you and anyone with you at risk of being possessed. Yes, this is right, an empty soul or something even more sinister can enter your body, mind, take you over. It has happened many times in the past, will keep happening while the board is allowed to exist. The Ouija board is a dangerous tool for attracting empty souls and sinister forces. My advice to you is not to get involved.

2 - Mental issues and psychosis.

People with mental problems are a target for empty souls. Which does not mean that every person with a mental health issue has got a demon walking around with them, or a ghost inside them - no way! But the point I make is: at times it is an acceptable hiding place for empty souls to get in and reside if there is willing compliance. In other words, the host soul has to be in total agreement with the empty soul invader. So there has to be expressed acceptance, permission, and it's not clear how this happens.

But when people have mental health issues and severe depression, soul energy levels hits an all-time low. The barrier defence mechanism goes down allowing conditions for violation. It does not occur a lot, don't panic, don't go looking at your partner or next-door neighbour just because they shouted at you or acted a bit strange. This situation, a rare occurrence in terms of ordinary life matters, but it does exist, and we have to front it, give you the lowdown.

3 - Drugs

Blowing your tiny mind with one too many of something in the drug department can let in empty souls. Let me first clarify something - no one is trying to preach regarding what you should be doing recreationally. If your spliffin it up to the eyeballs or taking more potent stuff that is up to you, people have a right to do whatever they feel. So no offence meant with this little piece of advice. Drugs, though, are the primary source or reason for empty souls violating a body. Blowing your brains out on coke one time too many can let in the lodgers. It all depends on the circumstances of where you are at timewise. The next storyline, a couple who enjoyed modern living and all the temptations that came along with it.

The story of a man who went to the well once too often concerning mind-bending, drug-fueled, blowouts. It's a frightening tale, but please note will only happen to 0.1% in any given lifetime. Listen and learn.

Marcella Rios Gonzalez is a beautiful black girl in her early forties. She was born in the Cayman Islands but now splits her life between the United Kingdom and Spain where she shares a villa with her partner Frank. Marcella has a degree in economics and is an equal shareholder in a private health care company based in London and Madrid. In a sense, has it all - brainy, beautiful, a businesswoman in her own right with a bag load of poise and dignity to go with it.

But not everything is right; there is something wrong - her partner Frank. Frank Roberts has been with Marcella for about ten years he is an English born guy who runs an accountancy business. Frank deals with a lot of high flying people all over Europe. His clientele range from the straight to the slightly not so straight - the criteria, though, easy enough. Frank saves them money his accountancy and business knowledge worth its weight.

Marcella thinks that of late Frank has changed. It's his attitude more than anything. He has always been an outspoken, volatile, high living guy who could flare up one minute and die down the next. But lately, there is some difference in his personality and Marcella can't quite get to the bottom of it. She's aware that he has to go on private business trips now and then and while on them there is a little added *playtime*. She is also familiar with the fact that *playtime* tends to centre around recreational drugs - such as cocaine. The truth is Marcella is absolutely on the ball. There is something not quite right with the guy and as the eternal fly on the wall - I will tell you exactly what it is.

He is more than just the occasional coke sniffer. He goes over the top and during one of the client get-togethers out in sunny Portugal - *Frank blows his brains out*. Easy enough when the champagne and caviar take over, laced with a little light music, and served with a couple of nubile swingers both under twenty sat opposite with legs akimbo.

As the days go by the tension between Frank and Marcella builds up. It's not only that he flares up every five minutes. it's the garbage he tends to spew. "You're a fucking cock sucker with benefits, you bitch. You're only here for the money. If I had fuck all, you'd be gone Marcella, and you know it." Mmmm, loud, aggressive stuff and not like this guy - not usually. Plus there is something else worth a mention.

When Frank is not sounding off, he sits in his room with the television on low. Now a lot of you will raise a few eyebrows over this one; it's not quantum physics Why shouldn't a guy like Frank sit and watch what's on the box - breaks up the monotony? True, but it's the quality of what he's watching. Old fashioned black and white 50s romance movies. Or old biddy stuff like Lunchbox with the late *Noele Gordon*, all in black and white. For pity's sakes, this is a guy in his early forties, a high flying accountant - not the sort of thing you expect.

There is one other nightmare worth mentioning It's Franks driving - crazily fast. The car, a top of the range Mercedes, smart, practical, a decent enough money car to show your clients you are not on the breadline. Now Frank's never been a slowcoach when it comes to cruising through the streets of Madrid but of late, hectic stuff at breakneck speed. He jumps several red lights and goes through a crossing nearly knocking down an old lady. How he's not been pulled over by the *Guardia Civil* I do not know.

There's one particular incident which sticks in the craw, certainly for Marcella. Driving like a complete maniac late in the evening, Frank barely avoids hitting a woman and her young son in a narrow street. He swerves violently causing a huge screeching sound and stench of burning rubber. Marcella is at her wits end. "You idiot Frank, you nearly killed that woman and her boy." The air turned blue for the next forty seconds. "So fuckin what they should not be out this time of night - pair of dickheads."

Marcella winces takes a deep breath before replying. "You can't carry on like this you're going to kill someone before too long. Either that or you'll blow the car up. Look at yourself, driving like a complete idiot, can't wait to trash his engine - and for what. How in God's name did it get like this what's happened to you?" The air is blue, Frank makes it bluer. "Cars like these were made to be raced and trashed just like the women who sit in them, do nothing but criticize. Believe me if I had an ejector seat for you - I would use it. No worries."

Not the best of scenarios, certainly not for Marcella Rios Gonzalez. She loves Frank and all his faults, but how much more punishment can she realistically take? Then on a business trip to London, an old friend, an Asian lady, Mona Sedero pops into Marcella's office for a chat. The two have known each other for years, and the conversation soon turns into lunch at Claridge's.

"I just don't get it Mona, can't grasp it. He was lovely and then bingo overnight changed into a monster. Fly's off the handle at anything and everything you say to him. Drives like a maniac. I cannot tell you how low and depressed it's making me." Mona looks in a bit of a dream world, she is though, being pensive, thoughtful, turning things over in her mind before speaking.

"There's this old man, a doctor, a funny old guy. He lives in Stamford, Lincs. I'm thinking deep, but I can't remember his name. Julie Gosh was talking about him only last week. Dr Zoom, that's it his name is Dr Zoom."

Marcella blinks seems to wake up. "Oh yeah, what does he do?" Well, I'm not sure, but he's like a mystic guy, a shrink of sorts does loads of different things. My friend Julie took her Brother Jaz to see him. Apparently, Jaz has some kind of nervous disorder or twitch, makes him afraid of people and things. This guy Zoom cured him. Don't know what he did, but my friend's brother is a hundred per cent improved. Do you want me to get his address and number - do you think it could help." Marcella nods, "yes, get it for me Mona and thank you, honey - anything is worth looking into, **ANYTHING.**"

It's 11.00 clock in the morning, a typical Wednesday. Dr Paul Zoom PhD, Hypnosis (Stanford University USA) sits at his kitchen table coffee in one hand a pile of papers in the other. Outside his window, in the old fashioned Georgian courtyard, he can see wife Jean pegging out washing. It was the right move to make coming here. London, ok, but too overcrowded and claustrophobic for both of them. Stamford, a little old rural town stuck out in the middle of Lincolnshire, but there is breathing space here and fewer car emissions. The clinic he and Jean have set up is making significant strides, so many people who have Paranormal schizophrenia, need treatment. It doesn't look like they will make it back to the States for a visit this year - to many people to see and they are coming from all over Europe. In fact, today there is a compelling case due in from Spain, Frank Roberts accompanied by partner Marcella.

There is not a lot of information, but the case looks interesting regarding Miss Gonzalez's letter to him, and some of the behaviour patterns concerning Frank described within. This prospective case, a job for both himself and Jean, who as well as being his assistant, is DCH (Doctor of Clinical Therapy) trained.

The Cross Country train makes its way out of Cambridge station due to arrive at Stamford at 12.30 pm. Sitting together in the first-class rear end carriage, Marcella, and Frank who caught an early morning flight from Madrid to Stanstead airport. "I'm not sure about this guy." Says Frank, yawning slowly, trying to look relaxed. "I'm not certain what this regressive therapy thing is supposed to do for me or whether or not I should have allowed you to persuade me to give it a go."

Marcella, looking at him behind a set of dark glasses." Frank, we have little to lose or rather you don't. Those anti-depressants didn't work, not that I think you are depressed, but we are not getting anywhere. No one seems to know what's wrong. The doctors in Madrid don't. They believe there's nothing amiss with you, all down to anxiety and stress syndrome caused by overworking. The reviews on this guy are good; he comes highly recommended. I want the anger and mood swings to go, Frank - we have to give it a try."

After a short while, the train pulls into Stamford station where Marcella and Frank get into a taxi and arrive at Dr Zooms clinic well in time for Frank's appointment. Once the usual salutations and firm handshakes are completed both Frank and Marcella sit together in his office accompanied by Zooms wife, Jean. After a brief synopsis concerning the work of the clinic, procedures they use, there is a short forum of questions and answers.

Doctor Zoom initiates the dialogue. "Are you with it, Frank? Have you an understanding of what we are going to do here?" "I think so," says a sheepish looking Frank. "Correct me if I'm wrong, you intend to put me under and take me back to a state of consciousness where I disclose the beginnings of my anger issues. Is this right?" Dr Zoom looks him straight in the eyes. "The techniques we use here are groundbreaking. It's not just a case of putting you under. Yes, there is hypnosis, but to be fair, there is a great deal more. The intended plan is advanced MSA. Mind swap analysis."

Frank looking even more sheepish, twitches a bit on his chair which allows Marcella to jump in via the brief pause. "You get inside his head doctor - yes?" Zoom continues the dialogue. "With the help of Jean, my wife, who is a qualified hypnotherapist, we undertake to enter a part of the mind and memory. Try to get a clear picture of what's there. What is motivating the unusual anger patterns, changing the lifestyle. You Frank will be in one room - I in another. Both of us will be under hypnosis and seemingly in a deep state of sleep. Two nurses will oversee the procedure along with my wife, who takes the defining role as practice manager and head of nursing. The procedure, along with all other procedures at this clinic are one hundred per cent safe, certified, and governmentally approved."

Again, it is Marcella beating Frank to the draw, bolting in with a reply. "Doctor what do you think you will find inside him. Do you think Frank is possessed?" Doctor Zooms face takes on a stern look. "Sometimes, the aura wall becomes damaged, allowing free passage to the mind. As we have already discussed, lots of things can do it, and it's not clear in this case how it happened or whether or not it did happen. Franks got a problem he's not entirely himself. If he is sharing his space with something or somebody - then we need to know." The conversation ends, and without further ado, Frank Roberts accompanied by partner Marcella prepare for what I can only describe as a bizarre, strange, journey - his mind about to be breached by Doctor Zoom - **A SHRINK OF SOME MAGNITUDE.**

A clinic in sleepy little Stamford, Lincolnshire, where an unusual procedure is about to take place: in two separate rooms on a couch lying on their backs - two men both in deep sleep and trance. One of them is Doctor Paul Zoom, an expert regarding the more profound implications of the human mind - how to penetrate and explore.

Doctor Zoom wakes up or at least thinks he does. There is a strange feeling of light-headedness, shaky on the feet. *Where am I? he ponders. Need to focus ground myself, identify where I am at - my surroundings.* The terrain does not look familiar with anything rational. It seems like the Doctor is in a series of passages. The colour, grey to brown, and everything, dimly lit. There's a strange sound like the constant whirring of a generator. A weird noise and in a way it's like being somewhere enclosed yet a feeling the sea is just outside your window - you can hear the sound of crashing waves in the distance.

The tunnels, passages, wind on forever then out of the corner of his eye he notices something - A street sign with a name on it. **CEREBRAL ROAD**. *My sainted bottle of Budweiser how the hell did that get here*? A little further on there is another sign, **MEDULLA WAY**. *Ah, yes, I know where I am, he thinks. I'm in the brain, the temporal mind of Frank Roberts. I'm here.*

As Doctor Zoom continues along winding passages, he notices that every so often there's a small recess enclosing a door. In one such opening, a door with a sign on it and the name **DAWN**. *Interesting*, he thinks. *Not a place you would expect to find anyone living. Oh well, let's give it a knock see who's in.*

He raps the door knocker and waits. After a couple of minutes, the door opens, and a woman stands there. At a glance, you could easily place this lady in mid to late sixties. Her hair is in a style of a bun, and she appears a little overweight around her waist.

She has a soft round face and glasses and dressed in a frock. For all the world she might have stepped out of the 1950s - anyone's Grandma.

"Oh, you must be the landlord? I was expecting you come in." Dr Zoom steps through the door into a pokey little living room with one table, two chairs and an old black and white television set. He wants to talk, but before he can open his mouth, Dawn beats him to it. "Don't think I was trying to get out of paying. That's not my way, but no one came around to see me. No one has asked for any rent money." Zoom, taken back a little but soon regaining composure. "No not at all I don't want any money from you. I saw your name above the door and just got curious to see who was here." Dawns face breaks into a smile. "Oh, how lovely you've come to see me - the first person in thirty years. Oh, do take a seat and stay awhile, let me make you a cup of tea." Dawn disappears to make tea, allowing the good doctor a chance to look around the room.

On a shelf was a picture of Winston Churchill smoking a trademark cigar and giving the two-fingered salute that he often did. On the wall, snapshots of two young girls sitting on a seat in what looked like a busy town centre, possibly London in the late 1940s. The room was grey and dismal, could have done with a coat of paint to brighten it up.

The strangest enigma, though, the television set. It was ancient and looked like an early 1950s Rediffusion complete with massive tubes and wires poking out the back. My god a dinosaur if ever there was one. However, time for a nice cup of tea and a fact finding mission.

Paul Zoom sits back on a chair, takes a sip of the tea and starts speaking. "How long have you been here, Dawn?" "Oh," she says. "About a year, not too long for me." "And where were you before," he asks. "I lived with a man for over thirty years prior to here. In the end, he died, and I had to leave. He was a nice man who liked his own company; he got old with me. This one's nice never any bother. Like I say I thought you were coming for the rent I always pay my way." The good doctor looking quizzical; he's slowly beginning to piece this one together. *She's harmless god bless her but refuses to move on.* "What year did you pass Dawn?"

The strength of the question is enough to make Dawn jump. She looks distant, slightly embarrassed before answering. "Pass, what do you mean?" "When did you die?" Says Zoom. "How long back?" She looks down into her teacup for a good few minutes before raising her head, tears in her eyes. "I know I shouldn't have come here, but I didn't have anywhere to go the door was open and.." Dr Zoom interrupts her mid-sentence. "Take it easy I understand, relax and don't worry we can sort it out. Try and remember Dawn, the final day, if you can?" Dawn wipes her eyes, pain, and memories flooding back.

"It was in the early 70s I lived alone, similar to here in one room. One morning I woke up and could not move. I lay all day in and out of consciousness until in the end, I felt myself rise, saw myself looking down at me. I knew then I had died." Doctor Zoom puts his hand over Dawns, slips her a tissue from his pocket and continues the questioning.

"Light, was there light, brightness, did you see anything?" She dabs her eyes before replying. "Yes, there was light a tunnel of it - and a person." "A person!" Says Zoom. "Who was this person." "My sister. My older sister Debbie who died when I was ten. She was the only person I loved, but she left me - they all leave me one way or another."

Paul Zoom wiping his brow with a tissue; for some reason, the room is getting hot. Hardly surprising emotions running high in a small confined space. But it would be wrong to stop now. *I'm near to cracking this he thinks, gotta prize a bit more out of her.* "So, what happened with Debbie? Did she say anything, any close-knit dialogue between you?" "Yes" replies Dawn. We talked; briefly, she was so pleased to see me, held on to me would not let go of me. Debbie wanted me to leave with her, she held my hand and said we should go quickly. Others were waiting for us." "So why didn't you go what stopped you?" Dawn looked down at her hands; fidgeting didn't seem to know what she should do or say. "I was afraid. I could't take it all in, my big chance to get away and I refused it when the time came. I just felt I needed to think things over - dwell on it, work it all out. Before I realized, years had gone on, I found myself living as I had always lived - alone."

Doctor Zoom shifting a little in his seat, looks at Dawn deep into her eyes, far into her mind before speaking. "You can't stay here, Dawn. You have to move forward towards the light. Debbie will still be there, still waiting for you. You will not be alone, I promise." She looked slightly relieved before replying. "Could I still go then, they would have me after all of this? I mean, I'm willing to try again. Speaking to you after years of nothing gives me hope, something to inspire me. It could be alright, couldn't it? This time I can do it - get away from this place."

Doctor Zoom smiles in a relief-like way before answering her. "They will be delighted to have you. It will be much nicer than here and so many new people waiting to meet you, talk to you. In many ways, you're a bit of a celebrity." She laughs. "Me a celebrity, how?"

"Not many people can hack this plane of existence as you have." Says Zoom. "You subjected yourself to a life of permanent self-denial and frugal circumstance. Dear lady, as far as I'm concerned, you are a paragon of virtue. No one in this Universe will ever deny it." "Thank you for that." whispers Dawn, tears once more beginning to well. "Please tell the landlord I will send him some money. I didn't mean to walk into his mind without permission. But I needed somewhere to stay, just for a while. I hope he understands?" "I know him well says Zoom. He's a good guy he won't hold it against you." With that, they both stand up and approach each other. Doctor Zoom links his arms around Dawn and hugs her. "Dear sweet lady bless you infinitely through eternity and may the Universe grant you the power of love, unity, and friendship with those who hold you dear to them. Never again will you be alone."

At this point, it's hard to know what is happening. Light fills the room, and there is a marvellous scent of Lily of the Valley. Doctor Zoom cannot be sure but thinks he sees a young girl holding Dawn's hand, her sister maybe? We shall never know, the light reaching intensity and then - vanish! He leaves the room, closing the door gently behind him. As he walks, he pauses, looks back at the door. A small burning cross has replaced the name Dawn and there is a feeling of relief. **Hallelujah** she's made it.

Paul Zoom, once again in the winding passages of Frank Roberts dislocated brain. Back on the bubble and tripping the light fantastic as he winds his way through endless turning corridors, the whirring sound of a generator type noise in the background. After a while, he feels he hears something. Something different, faint at first and then becoming louder - it sounds like a man shouting at the top of his voice in the distance. *"I will fuckin kill you."* As Doctor Paul Zoom gets nearer the shouting becomes louder. **"I WILL FUCKIN KILL YOU."** Another small recess appears and a door. On it, the name **DANNY MICHAEL MURRAY**, next to it stands the words **THE ACCUSED**. Before Doctor Zoom can ponder the more profound implications of the situation, the door flies open and there stands a man. He's odd-looking, a white guy probably English age about nineteen to twenty-six. He is tallish, lanky looking, a mop of mousey hair and a pinched shrew-like face. To be honest, he looks disgustingly evil, like a sicko dork but as Zoom, and rightly so, contemplates in his mind - *I'm not the one to make judgments.*

The guy suddenly speaks or rather booms it out like a foghorn. He's got a slight cockney accent. "Whadda you want? And who sent yer? Was it him? Mr Smart-arse landlord. If it was, **I WILL FUCKIN KILL YOU."** Paul Zoom has been around a while, but he will need all those years of experience to handle this funny bloke. "No sweat Danny I can see your point but let's have a chat over it, see where we stand." Foghorn Danny as I shall call him grabs hold of Doctor Zooms arm and fair yanks him through the door and into a large spacious room.

The guy's pad is so different from the place that housed Dawn. It is big and well decorated, candelabra dangle from the ceiling and there is a small bar in the corner. Foghorn Danny leers. "This is what akkers can get yer when you got Venezuelan connections. Anyway, What do you wanna chat about? He sent yer, didn't he?

Mr landlord sent you to put the frighteners up me, yeah? Well I got news, fresh evidence. I got new stuff that my lawyers will be takin to the Old Bill soon. I'm gonna clear my name and until I do that fuckin cunt won't get a fuckin penny out of me. Ok, that's what I say let's hear what you gotta say."

Old Zoomy boy usually knows the score, but this a strange case - a funny one. *I need to know more about this guy he thinks. So better stay on the right side of him. Get the low down, get to the heart of it.* "Danny it sounds pretty interesting what you're saying. But I'm not in the picture fully. What do you mean about lawyers and clearing your name?"

Danny Murray's face takes on a long, lean, popeyed look to it. He speaks frantically. "The girl, he killed her. The little girl he mowed her down in his Porsche and fitted me up with it." "I see," says Zoom. "So, what happened to you?" "The Old Bill arrest me and stick me away for something I don't know nuffin about. But I got new evidence. I got new stuff that will clear my name. I can't be framed, can't be kept down, **I WILL FUCKIN KILL YOU AND IM** if you try it."

A real enigma this but when Danny turns his back to fix a drink Doctor Zoom sees something out the corner of his eye. A newspaper cutting is lying on a chair. The headlines read: **'HIT AND RUN KILLER DIES OF MASSIVE HEART ATTACK IN CUSTODY.'** *Mmmm, he thinks. This little gem of information ought to throw some light on matters. I'll base the angle of attack on this info - see how far I get with it. Also, I can Google him.*

"But Danny listen, why did the police think it was you? Why did they arrest you for something you didn't do?" Danny Murray, face contorted like a pug-faced Pekinese is quick to retort. "Your mate is in league with the Old Bill. He paid em off. I was unlucky enough to be in the area that night when it happened. Plus I killed a bird or something - a pigeon flew into the screen. Perfect stitch up material for mister fuckin landlord and his bent copper mates. **I WILL FUCKIN KILL IM AND YOU** and anyone else trying to set me up for stuff I didn't do."

It's becoming increasingly evident what has happened - what

went down here so to speak. Doctor Paul Zoom knows it or thinks he does. Danny Murray killed a little girl. He mowed her down while driving like a maniac - probably high on coke or something similar. The guys in total denial but not just that a child's death has come about through his negligence. He's snuffed it himself and doesn't know it. Or if he does, will not admit to it. *More likely to be the latter thinks* Zoom. *But how do I get him to confront his problem?*

"Ok, Danny what now? What do you intend to do now?" Danny, perplexed looking starts shouting, **"FUCK ALL.** I'm doing nuffin and going nowhere until he admits. I will build my case until your mate confesses to murder. That's what I'm gonna do - what would you do?" Doctor Paul Zoom looking intense, severe, in the face and eyes. He leans over as close to Danny as he dares. "You could always go to the light."

Danny looking puzzled. "What fuckin light? What you on about?" "Your dead" says Zoom. "Your dead Danny, you died in custody, a heart attack, one too many snorts up the sniff box." With this statement, he grabs the newspaper, cutting and sticks it under Danny's nose." "That's you Danny the report of your death as it appeared in the papers. Your gone baby and you have to face it - walk away Danny, move on." By now, Danny's angry, and it's beginning to show. "What you saying you fuckin wanker? Oh, I get it your mate thinks he can send me a smart-arse Preacher boy - frighten me out. I'm not moving on, and if you try anything, **I WILL FUCKIN KILL YOU."**

"That won't be necessary, Danny," says Zoom looking pensive. "There's enough died already without adding to the list. Dan, you have to go, it's the only option open to you. You cannot stay here." *He's a stubborn one this thinks Zoom, won't lie down.*

Danny Murray proving harder to shift than oven grease. But Doctor Paul Zoom has one ace left in the pack - which he now delivers. "Your right, of course, I can't make you leave, but I know some people who can!" Danny the Murray man, sneering a reply. "Yeah, who?" **"THE NUNS"** says Zoom. I'll send in the **NUNS."** Danny pauses, looks slightly stirred but not completely shaken if you get my drift. Then laughs out loud. "So fuckin what they're all dead." "You remember them then? Remember how they brought you up in the East end of London when you were a child." "I remember but they're all fuckin history, gone, six feet under. Dead people can't hurt yer," he sneers. This half-baked confession is the moment our hero doctor has been waiting for, and he dives in for the kill like a human razor blade.

"Oh but Danny they can, dead people can affect you in a big way - especially if they are dealing with someone as **DEAD AS THEY ARE!** I'm sure sister *Magdalena Montero Delagousta* would love to know your whereabouts."

The outcome of this statement is nothing short of instant. For the first time, Danny Murray looks frightened, like he had just seen a ghost if you can forgive the pun. "You and your fuckin mate won't get rid of me. I will be back, and I w*ill fuckin kill you."* This time though, the delivery of speech and the effect it produces seems lower in tone. *Unbelievable* thinks Zoom. *Amazing what a bit of Goggle box and Googling can achieve when your backs to the wall. Now, i lay the ghost.*

From a fly on the ceiling perspective, I doubt that Danny Murray will ever appear in the mind of Frank Roberts again. Once you rid the spectre - it never comes back. At least to the same body. But this is a personal viewpoint I have no concrete proof. Back to an unusual scenario, playing out in another man's mind. Once Danny knew the score - he completely disappeared. Walked away, gone in a flash, leaving Doctor Zoom sitting all alone in the departed soul's front room. Our good Doctor, tired, stressed out to the point of collapse. Without further thought, goes into the bedroom that once belonged to a ghost - gets beneath the covers and sleeps.

Some hours later a high-speed train heads towards Cambridge carrying a host of passengers. Among them Marcella Gonzalez and Frank Roberts. Franks treatment at Doctor Paul Zooms clinic a perfect one or seemingly so. He awoke from a trance-like state after approximately an hour - never felt better.

He certainly feels no immediate anger in his mind. He's calm and collected like he used to be. Dr Zoom, not giving much away regarding the outcome, what had happened while Frank slept. Only to say that everything had gone well - mission accomplished, and Frank was clear of any negative influences and reactions. Again, though, giving little information on what those negative influences were, the methodology used to rid them. At the minute, though, this is hardly an issue, and Frank and Marcella are just happy to relax, chill out on the train. Marcella is taking the chill aspect one step further by plugging in her notebook to the trains Wi-Fi system and booting up. It's time to look for a holiday. "Oh, my goodness." She shouts. "Oh my, where did this come from?"

Her sudden startled behaviour causing Frank to show an interest. "What's wrong?" "Someone's left me a strange message. Oh my God, look at this" "What is it" says Frank. "What does it say?" Marcella angles the notebook so he can see a clear view of the screen. On it in massive capitals and blood red in color -

'I WILL FUCKIN KILL YOU.'

CHAPTER 10 - SUICIDE DON'T WORK

Suicide does not work. It will not do what ninety per cent who are committed to it expect. It is a futile gesture. The of people who commit suicide are of the mindset that once dead - that's it, no more worry or pain regarding whatever issues they experienced in life. This viewpoint a mistaken one, in the sense of, the problem remains. All that happens, you switch dimensions but the issues, difficulties, still there. Still staring you in the face - no escape. So instead of getting out of it by killing yourself, it becomes worse. The soul racked by guilt. The guilt of having quit on life and condemned loved ones left behind. And this is what you do when you commit suicide - damn yourself to remorse, condemn those left behind who mourn you.

On the other hand, there seems to be a misconception surrounding suicides in general. Some of the things I hear make me cringe. Some people suggest to me that by committing suicide, you go straight to hell, ending up in some form of the burning pit. Waist-high in boiling oil, screaming for mercy. Forget it, man. This garbage doesn't work - never in a million years, the stuff of infantile thinking, guaranteed to scare the wits out of you, nothing more.

When you take your life, the higher realms help you deal with it, they do not punish you. In a way, no one blames you. In the spiritual life, there is an understanding of why people do it. There is knowledge surrounding the mentality behind it. As souls, we should never have come to the earth plane - the earth, not an ideal life for the expression of the higher self.

For a start, the soul does not get old, if anything rejuvenates as it grows. The body though, ages and becomes decrepit. In this lies the main reason souls do not get a fair deal on planet earth, they age and cannot stand it. Some people will stand all day telling you different. I do not believe it. I repeat souls cannot stand ageing -

the biggest nightmare. The reason they cannot stand it, because in the higher world it does not exist, it's never existed since the dawn of creation. Souls are pure, angelic-looking. When they come here, they take on the ugliness of humanity, and it doesn't suit.

But there is more. When souls are born into earth life, they exist under penalties, laws governing the existence of living in a body. The world we exist in here, a box, a prison, entrapment whatever way you look at it. We are not free in this life; we like to think we are. But the truth is the opposite. In earth life, we remain trapped until we leave our bodies upon death. When you evolve from a higher source but take on the penalties of lower consciousness, it's easy to come unstuck - for instance, the entrapment of debt.

Nobody should be in debt. In the sense of, the repayment obligation should never exist in life. But it does and causes untold misery to millions of people. Why? It's down to laws governing planet earth, circumstances, and karma. It's easy to say that we should never get into debt. But we all know, it's impossible to avoid. I mean, we could go on all day trying to analyse. But the main consensus - debt in material life is unavoidable.

In the higher consciousness, there is no such thing. There is no need for money in the higher realms. Everything you need in the spiritual world comes through manifestation - of which we can all do. Though as I have explained in other areas of the book. Some are better at it than others. In the higher life, they are debt-free because there is none. In the lower, it is a massive issue causing, stress, anxiety, worry and sometimes suicide. So you can see how easy it is to kill yourself, get out of these problems - or so you think. In the higher world, they know the issues we go through. They have empathy with us, shake their heads and wonder just how we manage to stay a day on the planet, let alone a lifetime.

Some souls never come to the earth plane. They will not risk it, too hard, unstable, degrading. There are higher Angelic forces who have never been to the earth and will never do so. After all, why should they? The higher life is perfect if you compare it to what we have here. The life here is a frightening one full of risk and circumstance. Living here is unfair, simply because the rules and regulations that make up the world are open to manipulation. On planet earth you are cheated, it's an orchestrated world designed to fit one individual rather than a group. It is the only life where you can work yourself silly and never get rewarded.

However, even though existence here is hard and higher Angelic forces do not want to be here. They secretly are in awe of us. For human souls to come to this world and take the worst of what is on offer leaves their halo's lopsided. We are a special breed of soul, earmarked for something of a super divine quality once we have been through our baptism of fire. The higher Angelic forces know this and because of it, hold us in high esteem. In the next chapter, a story about a man who thought he could buck the trend of living, get away from his problems - a guy who ends his life in the hope that all issues will vanish into thin air. Only to find they are beginning.

SUICIDE - ALAN SELEKARS STORY

Alan Selekar is a car showroom manager. He works for a successful auto sales franchise in North London, their top salesman before becoming a boss. To be fair and honest, Alan is as obnoxious as they come. A corporate assassin, twenty-five years of age, married with one child. His style of management beggar's belief in today's politically correct marketplace.

"Yer need to close the fucker - now, idiot. Don't wait for next week. Get his fucking signature on that lease **NOW!** Whadda mean you can't, he's not ready to go ahead. Listen *Numb Nuts* you're the one who'll be going ahead. Headfirst straight through the bloody door - sacked!" Personally, in the long run, I can't see his style of management flourishing. But In today's boss-controlled climate, untold amounts waiting for a job - any job. Then you begin to realise, hey he just might get away with it.

Alan's at a crossroads, he's been working in a showroom in the centre of London for five years where he presides like *Adolf Hitler* at the Reichsprasidentenpalais in Berlin. The company though, want him to take over their new place just outside of Wolverhampton in the West Midlands. It's a daunting task, but

Alan is super cocky, sure he can hack it anywhere in the world.

"I can sell sprats to an effin mackerel if you base me on Baffin Island" he once told his area manager. The knobhead fancies himself crazy, *Gordon Bennett*, Baffin Island for god's sake - what porno comic did he get that piece of information? After several interviews, they do a deal. Alan and his family, wife Marina and seven-year-old daughter Ariadne will move to the outskirts of Wolverhampton, where Alans biggest challenge of his career awaits him. It's here at this juncture; things take a turn.

Alan interviews and takes on a girl, Lisa Cooper. She comes on board as finance manager. Lisa's a twenty-something, over the top platinum blonde with a full set of film star veneers, goofing elasticated jaws and an ample sugar-coated grin. Couple that with a size six figure straining to exit a trouser suit - you gotta pocket battleship of an ego. Pozzo! Once she starts at the new showroom, Lisa and Alan become inseparable. *Adolf Hitler,* suddenly finding his *Eva Braun.* But here is the crux of the matter - it's not gelling sales-wise.

The figures, not picking up. Alan's brand of management, not working. The reasons clear enough. Most of the sales team in London were young guys all under thirty. Alan's bullying tactics registered with these. Perhaps it was because company policy brainwashed them into believing sales is like this - the boss degrading you to get the figures.

Whatever the mindset, it matters not. Alan is not motivating his team; car sales are pants. Plus, there is something else. Lisa is now Alan's bit on the side. The whole world and his dog know about it but the two not bothered in the slightest. In fact, they hold hands in the showroom at every available opportunity - not suitable for staff morale.

Then, at an office, social, night out in Birmingham, there's an incident. The sales team sit in a swishy upmarket restaurant in the centre of Brum. Lisa, drunk as a lord and swearing at the top of her voice. "Oh yeah, that dickhead Martin couldn't sell fish to a fuckin penguin. Oh, and lazy git Kim, 'fat bastard,' I hate him." Not entirely professional, slagging off your sales team on a night out in a posh diner. It gets worse, Lisa smashed up to the eyeballs on *Pornstar Martini's* makes a massive fundamental, kamikaze error. Slags off Alan. "Oh he was a trainee, I brought him up to scratch - kicked his balls, the 'arsehole'." Mmmm, yes, well, ha, ha' very funny Lisa providing you have an understanding guvnor with a warped sense of humour sitting next to you. Not paralytic *Genghis Khan* blotched up in a Champagne and Guinness ego.

"Go home you fuckin orrible slag." Alan's reply. "Go on fuck off home and take that sidekick floozy with you." I think by that he meant Monica who was unlucky enough to be the showroom receptionist. Either way, both girls made a fast exit. Lisa bawling her eyeballs, Monica looking like she'd just seen King Kong's dongler. Point being - not suitable for motivating a sales team. I don't feel the right principles of management designed to get more sales appropriately used here. But it resonated in one sense. Made the guys realize just who they were dealing with - two dickheads of the highest order.

One who thinks he's a manager then decides he's not - but goes back on it after ten pints of snakebite and two plates of sick. The other, a silly little, middle management, flyweight. All Botox and trouser suit. Pulled off the sidewalk cos she had a shapely rear end (bound to get deals). The truth is, she's missed her vocation - blow jobs down a blind alley more to the taste. In many ways, the disastrous night in a Birmingham diner, a catalyst of doom regarding Alan Selekars career.

The writings on the wall for our Al, the hell night in Brum setting precedence. Everything downhill from this point onwards. Lisa, still number two, does not trust him anymore, secretly wanting a dismissal so she can cash in. The sales team full of disdain. *'The sooner we get rid of this Wanker, the better'* the general, overall viewpoint. While on the home front just as gruesome. Wife Marina, threatening to leave and take the daughter. It's all falling apart, which goes to show. One minute your up there. King ego balls, lord of your own personalised dunghill. The next, normality returns, still flesh and blood.

THE END WHEN IT COMES - RUTHLESS!

"I'm sorry, Alan. The company want you to leave immediately - like now!" Richard Knightsbridge, area manager, grim in the face waiting for the obvious reply. When delivered, slightly stammered, nervy. "Hold on I've been with them for years since I left school. Come on, Rich, you know me just need a bit of time. I'll sort it." Knightsbridge a hardened old conker of thirty- five virtually spits. "It's not worked out Mr Selekar. The company have lost faith in your ability to deliver. We will pay you four months advance salary plus any entitlements. I have a cheque here." In the background, two burly security guards appear suddenly - the last Funeral Frogmarch about to take place in front of a packed audience. There you have it, the corporate killing machine takes no prisoners. Sell or be sold down the river. The truth of what we already know. You're as good as your last deal, nothing more. And regardless of any pontificating, bookselling, coin mongering, free trading, spunk filled, mind guru brainwasher. You're just a single stat in some distant, remote, junk-yard galaxy. Head office don't give a bollox! *If God didn't want them milked - why did he make them cash cows?'*

Now all stand while we sing the universal corporate national anthem - Ode To a Spent Arsehole. (Reppus Rustus). *"I ain't got no accreditation I can't get no plasticization. Though I tried and I tried, but it never worked out "* A little too pickety pop conscious for my own good - but I make the point.

Back to dear Al or what's left of him, sitting on the edge of the bed head in hands. No sign of Marina and Ariadne. Departed this morning to visit Marina's Mother - can't see em returning. The great UK business building dream ends up in the garbage can. Mortgage payments due and no prospect of further employment. Certainly, nothing on the scale of car showroom manager. There is a feeling of extreme hopelessness and pending depression.

But it does not materialise. Before it can get any worse, Alan decides to end it - kill himself. Death by hanging. *Let's face it he thinks, once I'm gone that's it no more pain or worry. I'll be out of it free, forever. I'm no use to anyone.* Knotting about twenty ties together, some of them given by the company, Alan hooks them around a giant masonry nail banged into the wall. Slips a noose around his neck and dangles. Within minutes there's a blackout - in the words of the immortal *Roy Orbison - 'it's over.'* He's dead, gone, kaput - but is he? Alan is still conscious in his mind. Perhaps it didn't work. There's one way to find out. Just wait until someone comes. *If I'm dead*, he thinks, *they will walk right through me.* For all his philistine habits, Alan Selekar is showing signs of underlying spirituality - perhaps he wasn't such bad a guy. Suddenly out of the blue, the doorbell rings. There at the entrance, a man who Alan recognizes instantly - his dad Norman. Oh well, he must be dead then. Dad died ten years ago.

Aftermaking a massive fuss of each other Alans dad starts to speak. "You did it then Al you got out." Alan looking puzzled. "What do you mean?" "Your dead our Alan," says his dad. "But to be fair none of us over here thought you would do it. We all felt you would hang about the earth life and sort the mess out that end - not this way."

"Wait a minute," says Alan. "What do you mean? There is no mess to sort out. I'm history, out of it completely. Dad, I'm dead. No worries." A sad, vacant expression appears on the face of Norman. He looks like he's struggling with his words. But they come out all the same. "Yes, true, your dead my boy but the problems have not gone away. You still gotta deal with em."

Norman puts his arm around his son's shoulder. "But listen, there is no need to worry. We are gonna help you in every way we can. Heal you up and make it better over time." Alan is not convinced. *Why am I being told all of this* he thinks. *I killed myself to get away from all issues - I'm surrounded by them still.* "Listen to me dad; I'm gone no one is gonna miss me. I failed them all. But I'm dead now that's it, freed everyone up from the pain of having to tolerate me." **POOR FOOL IF ONLY YOU REALIZED.** If only you knew the gravity of your actions. Not just to you but others connected to you. The scene changes suddenly, without warning, Alan and his dad are at a funeral. Both of them standing looking on while proceedings unfold. "You know who's in the coffin, don't you Alan?" says

Norman. After a pause, Alan replies. "I guess it's me." "Yes, it's your funeral but look a little closer, see who else is there." Alan looks close; there he sees Marina dressed in a black outfit head down, crying softly into a handkerchief. She looks devastated, supported by her Mother and Father either side of her. But where is Ariadne? Alan scans the church, looking for his daughter. Surely, she is here somewhere.

"Don't look for her Alan" says Norman. "She's not here. She isn't well enough to attend." "Why not?" Alan looking surprised. "What's wrong with her, where is she?" Norman, serious in attitude, takes a step back before answering. "The shock of your death affected her badly. She was the one who found you hanging from the top of the wall in the dining room. It affected the poor child's state of mind, Alan; she will be mentally ill for a long time because of it."

The ghost in Alan Selekar glows with an eerie brightness. The shock news concerning daughter Ariadne a little too much to bear. "But how dad, how did it affect her so badly?" Norman, Alan's dad, breathing deep before replying. "Why not, why shouldn't it? You see it from your angle - not Ari's. The human mind, a chaotic monster or can be if it is allowed to run away with itself. In Ari's case, it blew her head. Finding the daddy, she adored hanging from a masonry nail. Come on Al try seeing it from the other side of the fence."

Alan winces, stumbles, regains his composure. "Oh my god, what have I done. What have I done to my baby girl? Oh god, oh no, oh no. What about Marina dad, will she recover, will she be ok?" Norman looking strained, put out. Here was a man on a journey he did not want to complete.

"Well, yes, in a sense. But there is something I have to tell you. Something I know will cause great pain to your emotions. But I have to divulge. Have to say, or there is no way of healing you later."

Alan looking puzzled. "What, what is it? Call it." "Well, though, not yet aware - Marina's pregnant with child. Your child and it's a boy." Alans face for the first time in ages offers the grimace of a smile. But before he can take it all on board, the dad is back at him. **"SHE WILL NOT KEEP IT!** The pregnancy will be terminated."

"No, No, it can't happen. No, my son has to be born. No dad this is crazy why can't she keep it?" Norman Selekar feigns composure. The task of enlightening his son not an easy one. Has to be done though. "No chance her keeping it. Your death has created a knock-on effect, first guilt, then depression, finally anger. Every time she visualizes her son, she'll see you. She knows it in her mind, freaks her to the point where termination becomes the only logical outcome. You see the truth is Alan and I hate to say it like this - you killed yourself. But in doing so took your family along with you. You snuffed out their feelings to the point where guilt, anger, remorse, and pain do a really bad job on the soul. You, **CORRUPTED BOTH OF THEM** with a form of psychosis, heavily laced with depression. But like I said to you earlier we will try to put it right. There will always be a second chance. You can come again, get it fixed.

Alan's mind, one mass of emotional flux, deep resonating reflection. How could it turn out like this? How? I thought I was doing the right thing, setting them free, releasing them of the burden that was me. I didn't want it to be like this; I didn't want to hurt them. Why did I do it? I must have been out of mind. Oh god, why didn't I think? Why didn't I think straight? Why? The room Alan stood in takes on a strange shade of haze and blue. All of a sudden, tiredness comes over him. He closes his eyes and sleeps.

"Alan, wake up. Wake up, Al." The twisted gargoyle of a head that is Alan Selekar stirs under a blanket. Like a ninety-year-old codfish, open-mouthed, surfaces from the depths of the abyss and blinks. There above looking frantic wife, Marina. Alans puckering codfish lips start speaking.

"OH MY SAINTED FUCKIN ARSENAL. Where the Gordon Bennett am I? Is this hell?" "Will be," says Marina. "If you don't get down to Parkers in Wolverhampton by nine o clock. They got a job for you - senior car salesman. I spoke to your boss and the moneys brilliant. What you done to your ties Al knotting em together like this? They look a bit daft round your neck. What you been up to

Alan?"

A sheepish Alan takes time before answering. "Oh, nothing baby, nothing. A dream, silly ideas in your head. A plan you thought would work-no bottle to stick yer neck out and give it a go, complete the mission. And that's it really."

CHAPTER 11 THE UNIVERSE, THE FUTURE, THE DIVINE OBJECTIVE

There is one definitely! The idea is to bring matter and spirit closer together in balanced amounts. Create Heaven on Earth an eternal *Garden of Eden syndrome.* This plan means massive changes concerning how things work on the planet right now. There has to be a shift, vibrational change, taking us into a higher dimension yet still retaining an element of the material world, bringing the two in harmony.

Let me explain. Life on Earth is three dimensional, all about matter, solid earthy stuff. It's ninety per cent materialism and ten per cent spirituality. It is what it is; we can't change it, and there's no way out. People on the Earth plane (all of us) follow the material and physical viewpoint while trying to further our spiritual side.

The trouble is, we are up against it. Circumstances cause the material to overrule the spiritual. Ninety per cent of us living on Earth would like to see a better world. A world where people got fed properly, could pay bills quickly, afford to buy a house - a world where greedy utility companies stopped squeezing us. Where the justice system appears more to support more victims instead of criminals, where cases can be dealt with quickly. Where greed and monopolism is not allowed to take precedence over people's simple pleasures - such as television.

There are loads more issues. I have only scratched the surface. All of these things though, and more, stop spirituality developing. The world is as material as hell and *global powers that be* wanting to keep it that way.

We need help. We can only get it through divine intervention. The divine plan for the Earth plane is to lift it higher. Ascend the Earth into a higher dimension, eliminating the social injustices that have been allowed to flourish. What will be the changes in life? Time gets quicker and people, situations, respond. You do not feel that there are twenty-four hours in a day. You get to a point where it feels like a twelve-hour day. People get faster. They think quicker, talk like lightening - the body changes.

When the masses start to gravitate to a higher level of thought, it affects the matter, excites atoms, changes things. We look different. The body over a while becomes a light body as opposed to the dense version of now. A light body where energy as much as anything courses through the veins. There is still blood and organs, of course. But they function in a slightly different way, self-rejuvenate when things start to go wrong. With a more spiritually inclined body, the diet changes, people start to eat lighter food, meat disappearing off the menu for good.

Even methods of getting rid of body waste change. It becomes a more comfortable, delicate, more natural way to eject from the system. Like a short whistle of wind as opposed to a massive daily mud grind - loo roll a figment of the imagination. The higher ascended body combined with the lower allows for a longer life span. People live up to three hundred years before wearing out, starting to show it. Even then, there will be a rejuvenation program in place. You need not entirely die unless you want to.

In the higher version of life on earth, social injustices disappear. Murders disappear, people thinking on a raised level, going beyond this sort of behaviour. People's ability to self-manifest will see money all but go. It will be a case of barter between people than actually forking out large sums of cash. People trading skills. *You do for me - I do for you, so to speak.* Transport will be self-generated, in terms of people harnessing their soul energy, teleporting themselves from A-B in seconds.

A bit like something out of a *Star Trek movie* where you beam up. The higher definition of life on planet earth safe. No room for people whose mindset revolves around, robbery, fraud, murder, and mass destruction of people. Crime, more misdemeanours rather than wholesale criminal activity. If you are wondering how evil will is dealt with in the higher world. Well, those with murder on their mind - will not be allowed to ascend. And if they do, then

I doubt they can stay in the higher vibration, because, they will manifest fear. Fear dumps them back down to a 3D life where they will undoubtedly feel more at home.

In the higher consciousness, people will be more spiritual. Psychics, Readers, Healers, and Holistic Therapists will be the Superstars of the new age order. They will be as crucial as Lawyers, people seeking recourse to readings and psychic information to gain the edge. In the higher order of living certain things, we have been used to will disappear. There will be no lower life order creatures like snakes, insects, rats. Cats and dogs will evolve as well as other human-friendly animals such as horses. But do not expect to see Pit Bull Terriers tagging along - they thrive on fear and violence. There is no room for them. Sports and fitness will do well, but some traditional games and pastimes will become extinct as people demand more in the way of mind play. Soccer and American Gridiron will probably live on because there is a strategy factor there as much as anything else.

Possibly, boxing and wrestling will die out. People are demanding more to life than just seeing someone beaten to death. In the higher world, people will lose interest in this kind of behaviour. Games of the mind will be the most popular, especially if there are skill and tactics behind them.

It's not hard to see where higher life ideology is coming from regarding earth changes. The perfect world, one where you feel and act in the physical. But at the same time have a higher life consciousness at the back of it. In the spirit world, it is all about thought and symbolism. In the physical domain, its solid matter, and physical actions. Put the two together in equal amounts, and you have the perfect utopia.

There is a lot of evidence on planet earth right now to suggest that an ascension process is already underway. Time is quickening and over the last thirty years, accelerating beyond belief. Study how people talk, compare it to the way they did in the 1960s. It's so fast you are hard-pressed to understand what people are saying. Go into any mainstream city store and listen to the garbled twang that whines from the office intercom. It would help if you had a quantum physics degree to get anywhere near an understanding of it. People are talking faster, driving faster, moving at the speed of light to what they did forty-odd years ago. What happens when the acceleration reaches a specific limit? You ascend. Move into a higher dimension, but unlike the death process, your physical body goes with you. Or at least to a degree. Of course, not everyone makes it. The mass majority will, some can't. Certain people have no chance of ascending - or don't want to. If you do not move up to the higher Spiritual New World Order, what happens? You stay on planet earth. In terms of, continue with the 3D way of life.

Eventually, the two worlds split from each other. It does not happen in a quick, immediate sense. For a short time, they connect by an invisible bridge, which allows those who are unsure, latecomers, a chance to come on board. The bridge effect, though, does not last forever. There is a time limit. Once complete, the dual world's part. The two dimensions existing in their own space - never more to meet.

What sort of people cannot ascend into a higher vibration? The category divides into two areas, those whose mindset revolves around evil and the production of fear. Others who exercise free will - they can't be arsed for want of a better word. But usually, the evildoers and fearmongers are the ones who fail. They cannot ascend for one straightforward reason - their thinking remains undeveloped. The mindset is low and unevolved. If they were to make the shift, it would not last, the reason being, their fears, way of thinking, dropping them back down into the 3D world. In other words, they will not be able to hack it. The higher vibration is not suitable for low minded beings whose wish is for, death, destruction, total mind control of others. They belong here in the third-dimensional life - it gravitates perfectly to their way of evaluating things. Perhaps one day they will be ready. It's their bag.

How will this happen? No one is sure of the time. People who write, know the subject, all with different viewpoints. One theory is people will suddenly disappear. In terms of, one minute they are here on planet earth - the next, gone, disappeared. If you browse the Internet, you can find a lot of information that relates to the subject. I cannot go with this particular theory. It smacks too much of Space Age fantasy. I cannot believe that one minute you are talking to someone - the next, gone, vanished into thin air. Yet, even in the Old Testament (Book of Revelations), there is a reference to it.

There is also something called *Rapture.* It's big in American circles and is very keen on the theory of people disappearing overnight - their loved ones awaking the next day and wondering what the hell's going down. Like I say, I cannot go with it. But this is my personal view; no one sure how it happens. I favour the slow indoctrinating method over some time - a slow absorbing ascension process. People will have time to consider the new ways. See for themselves, life-changing dramatically, a new world type of order cementing into place.

There is one other point of view that i have to tell you about. **SOULS ARE NOT REINCARNATING , NOT COMING BACK TO THIS WORLD.** Why? It goes back a little way in time, possibly to just after the First World War. Little by little the Universal Karmic pattern of re-entry has changed. Souls are staying over the other side of life, damming energies and resisting the reincarnation process. They are doing it because they know it is not worth coming here again. Not worth reincarnating into a world whose cards are already marked!

Universal souls are aware that there is a shift coming - they know! They know because in the higher life they are party to this information quite freely. In a sense, it's a clever strategy for them but equally dissapointing for us on the earth. The great souls who came and went freely through the ages have abandoned this life and because of it we suffer. The part these souls played out over years of karmic *come and go* - an enormous contribution. And if you have trouble understanding, then consider a few points that i now put to you.

Look at life right now, all the wierd and irrational things happening on planet earth. Look at the people going off their heads in a multitude of ways. Study the murders, rapes, and child abuse that is surfacing at an alarming rate. Look at Politicians, corrupt, liars and money grabbers. Look at Children - murdering each other. A lot of people say - 'it's always been there.' True, but not as deep-seated as it is now. Not by a long chalk. Study the 40s, 50s, and 60's and compare the almost tranquility of life to what is here at present.

Why? Why is it happening? It is happening because of the forthcoming shift (Ascension). When a planet ascends everthing living on the planet or that has ever lived has a chance to evolve. A chance to go forward and embrace a wonderful evolution. In regard to people it includes good and bad. We all have a chance. The situation though, creates problems. Before we can evolve we have to rid ourselves of past life trash - cleanse our karmic rubbish. Under normal universal law, it is done gradually over many lifetimes. In this situation though, the dropping of ones karmic penalties is happening at an alarming rate of speed - to fast for some people. They cannot cope so they crack, go off their heads and commit the unthinkable. Which can include, murder, rape, suicide,

ANYTHING.

But there is something else - more sinister, frightening and harder to understand. There is infiltration of the Earth plane. The infiltration, from two sources. Within the planet and beyond it. Like i said earlier, Ascension allows for both good and bad to evolve at the same time. When Mother Earth ascends all manner of things spring from within her like a porous discharge. Anything good or bad that ever existed upon *Gaia's* back is given the chance to make the shift. Thus, one of the many reasons we are being bombarded with so much evil right now.

Finally, there are negative forces within the planet and possibly from without - that do not want us (Mankind) to ascend. They do not want evolvement for people and they are frightened to death that we as a human race will finally awake and realize who we are. Why? They are frightened because they will lose control of us. Lose the power to manipulate and run us while they live like Supergods in their ivory towers lined with massive wealth - that we as humans have provided for them.

So, leading up to the *Great Shift* there will be a concerted effort to stop the light giving powers from reaching us - enlightening us with Cosmic knowledge. But it wont work! In fact, will fail dismally. The shift cannot be stopped the Earth has to evolve and no futile efforts to stop it happening from Governmental sources or outside infiltration will succeed.

I REPEAT - THE SHIFT WILL HAPPEN
AND NOTHING CAN STOP IT!

So the old ways are retreating, vanishing into the mists of time. Enlightenment and change will come, go ahead, and ninety per cent of the population will go with it. In the sense of, *go with the flow*, allow it to evolve without paying much attention - a painless Ascension. We all want things to change, crying out for a new way of doing things, living our lives in a safe, progressive spiritual environment. Like *Sam Cooke* used to sing back in the sixties - *'Change is gonna come.'* I'm sure those words will prove to be deadly prophetic.

CHAPTER 12- KARMA THE LAWS GOVERNING OUR UNIVERSE.

Karma, to me, is the lifeblood of the universe. It is an invisible force mechanism that works in conjunction with universal principles, shaping, determining, creating, rewarding, and punishing. Karma is the universe's judge and jury, at the end of the day, it either pays you or gives you a hard time. It is also circumstantial. Continually, repeating and replacing in a person's life. In some ways, it is like a machine on autopilot. It just goes ahead and does a job. There is no bad feeling, no preference either way. Karma is fair and logical. It works on sound universal fundaments, facts, and figures and cannot make a wrong decision.

Karma goes from one life to another modifying itself through time. In other words, it adjusts to the era of any situation or person. This modifying time principle is one of the most essential sides of the karmic process, one we know little about, never explained in detail. In a man or woman's life, it is a serialization, starting from one life and continuing to the next. A cycle of events, deeds, and happenings that reach a significant culmination at some stage during your life. We will talk more of this later.

WHAT GOES AROUND COMES AROUND - BUT DOES IT?

Not necessarily. I hear this a lot and to be fair - it bores me to death. Trust me; it's not a foregone conclusion. *What goes around does not always come around* for the simple reason - half the time It's not your fault or theirs. Not always in your hands, others involving you, doing things. You end up a victim. In as much as, people manipulate circumstances, get you to do something or go along with it. When in truth - you did not want to. It happens a lot. But people are good at hanging on to this well-worn phrase and if you fall into the trap of totally believing it - then you can end up sadly disappointed.

The terminology ought to change. It should read, *What goes around will come around - at some point.* Not always in one lifetime though - sometimes it takes several. How many times have you seen criminals progress in life? How many times have you seen them make stacks of money from illicit practices like drug dealing or selling dodgy goods with no guarantees and a fraudulent purpose behind it? And, even when sent to prison. How many times have they come out with free property and a bag load of benefits to support them. They do it again, and again, breaking the law, laughing in the face of the police and justice system.

This behaviour, not a good explanation of what Goes around comes around. You know it and so do I - it's depressing! But there is hope. The Universe can formulate a plan even though, the procedure may take several lives to achieve. The bad guy does get it, but not always when you and I want them to - **LIKE NOW.** You cannot rely on instant karma; it does happen, but not every day of the week. In fact, I will say *"instant karma* is a rarity in this life." Try and think about this. The karma will work out, not always in one life, though. Sometimes, it can take several.

KARMA REPEATS AND MODIFIES - ONE LIFE TO THE NEXT

This is an absolute fact. What you were in one life, you are in this. The Universe, though, modifies the karma. Structures it to fit the age. It is similar to the people you meet. If you were born in the Middle Ages, perhaps you were a merchant's wife, married to a man you loved. Then you as a soul will be born again into a future age and bring the person you adored back with you. If you were a woman, then it's likely you will come back and be her once more - your husband will be similar. He will reincarnate on to the Earth plane and meet you again - marry you as he did in that bygone age. Hey, it's not rocket science.

The Universe modifies the karma to fit the period - props change 1345 becomes 2045. You at soul level work out a plan with the Universe to fit into any time zone that you find yourself. The main message, that you learn from one life to the next - make progress try and get to the next level.

WHY DO WE REINCARNATE?

By universal law, if you affect something, interfere with it, then you bind yourself to that person, project, or situation. A good analogy would be the story of the British Empire. The greatest empire in the world went into countries and forcibly, changed their religion, took the money and raw materials which did not belong to them and executed all and sundry that got in the way. We, as British interfered, got involved when the truth is, we did not have to. The British bound themselves to many nations by force. Once you get mixed up with their lives, once you commit indiscretions, even of a minor sort - you become part of the karmic process of that person, group, country, and nation. In short, they own you.

  Though, you might think it's the other way around. A good way of envisaging it is to imagine a Spider's Web. If you're an insect and you fly in there without thought of what you are doing - you get caught. You land yourself in a mess that can be difficult to get out of, resolve. In fact, the chances are you will never get out. Karma is similar. Involve yourself with something that you should leave well alone - you fundamentally are bound.

  Meaning, you must continue to be part of the process until you sort out the problems you created - leave the situation as you found it. The examples cited here, idealistic ways of looking at it. In truth, though, far more complicated with more significant issues forming in time. The pit gets more profound, the karmic connection more binding. The process, to clear, get back to the source becomes massively elongated - can span aeons.

   In terms of souls coming to this life and experiencing their karma - it is the same thing. To understand why we must go back to the beginnings. Souls, thought beings, came to the Earth, and contemplated its potential for existence. Eventually, they entered the primitive habitat and got involved - albeit not deep at first. Over time though, they tied themselves to the karmic merry go round - having to be born, evolve, die, and eventually return later to continue the process. It might seem like a tragic set of circumstances - it is not. Even allowing for the fact that half the time, we don't want to be here - every existence puts us forward if only a little. In short, we go forward. If you want to read a bit more about this part of karma - consider the teachings of *Edgar Cayce* or read the *Tibetan book of the dead*. There are others too numerous to mention.

MODIFICATION AND SERIALIZATION

Karma repeats we know this. But what does the term, serialization and modification mean? In terms of, what are the more profound implications. For me to show how this works, I will need to create a scenario that I used in my book, *The New Age Karma Handbook.* In the book, there is a story about a Medieval Knight who lived around about the 1400s. He died on the battlefield, but the manner of his death, brutal and frightening, will show how it affected his future.

But, first up, let's deal with the Knight and his ending - show how the modification and serialization played out in his next incarnation. There is a bloody battle in the year 1485. The Knight cut down with an axe (halberd pike) that penetrated his skull, killing him instantly. They stabbed him in the back of the neck at the top of the spinal column. Now, consider what you have here. The body would consist of a crushed skull that would quickly fill with blood.

The blood would soon find its way out of the corpse through all the natural orifices available. This information is logic that we are talking about something we can understand to be right. In other words, not out of this world. It would have happened this way. The Knight himself would have died fast after the fatal blow - but what would he have felt?

How would that initial blow to the head have resonated within the Knight? Well, I suggest there would have been pain and momentary confusion, then death. I think it is logical to suggest it happened like this. Now, five hundred years later, a little boy of six gets nose bleeds for no apparent reason. The doctor is confused. Nothing is pointing to the boy being ill. But he keeps having bleeds in the night. All the GP can do is put it down to growing pains - can't be anything else. But there is more; the lad is finding school difficult and confusing. He cannot concentrate on the lessons, gets anxious and worried. He tries to get on top of things but cannot focus properly.

If this was, you reincarnated from the 1400s. Still, with the soul memory of an axe in your brain - you could understand what was happening. But of course, it's not like this no one has a clue, entirely in the dark.

This, then, the meaning of karmic modification and serialization. The Universe brought back the Medieval Knight of the 1400s and plonked him into a modern age. The situation continues from where it left off. The blood from the axe planted straight into the head - still trying to find its level, the momentary pain and confusion remains in existence. But, modified by the Universe to resemble something else.

Laziness, maybe, he cannot concentrate because he can't be bothered. There is always an excuse for it, ever a reason. You bring back your karmic circumstances from where you left off. The Universe modifies the situation to fit the age - it always happens, even on a daily, everyday life basis.

CAN YOU CONQUER YOUR KARMA - GET OFF THE WHEEL?

In short, **NO** - it's tough and requires you to be too perfect a person. Of course, not everyone will agree with what I have written here. According to what you read; all the *Ascended Masters* have done it. Well, ok, I am not going to answer back. It cannot be proved or disproved. But to my mind getting off the wheel of karma is virtually impossible. Simply, because, we cannot go through a day without making mistakes of some description - let alone a lifetime. The three-dimensional earth life is too imperfect for us as souls to conquer. In a sense, it is a prison planet. We will never be perfect enough to ascend from this life - we need help. The Universe needs to step in and help us get off the wheel. How will it do it?

For humanity to get off the wheel of karma, the Earth plane needs to ascend. We as human beings living off her back so to speak - need to go with her. In short, we need to aspire to a higher life. Mother Earth ascends and we go along for the ride. This divine plan is what needs to happen. But when is this event likely to take place? No one knows the exact time. Certainly though, over the next hundred years or so, we should be able to achieve it.

When I say ascend, I mean, gravitate to a higher dimensional form of thinking. We live in a 3D world. If we all rise to the higher life at roughly the same time - then humanity will be on a 4th and leading to a 5th dimension. The mindset changes, the body undergoes modifications and the karma process as we know it ends. Oh, and more point. Most of us will do it, ascend that is. At least 98% will make it - 2% probably will not or cannot.

Finally, a story to show how karma works in life. The story about a young black man, unusual, gifted, and very spiritual. A man who in 1803 was captured by white European slave traders and brought to England. This karmic example, the story of *Rubin Mind.* It was first published in the *New Age Karma Handbook* back in early 2015. The story reproduced especially for you in this publication. I hope you enjoy it.

CHAPTER 13 - THE PERFECT KARMA
THE STORY OF RUBIN MIND. PART 1

The day is a peerless one. The sun shines high in a cloudless sky, midday is fast approaching. You can see beads of steamy vapor just beginning to form in the forest. Trees achieve a glistening effect, as moisture and heat join together. The red hot sweat of the jungle will soon take over from the damp, early morning mists. There is a dense stillness in this part of the world. A beautiful part I might add. A region of West Africa - The Gold Coast. Better known today as Ghana. The year is 1803, and the area is still largely uncultivated and rugged in its appearance. Many tribes exist along the coast, along with a sprinkling of Portuguese and Dutch settlers.

Enter, Rubin Mind the principal character in our story. Rubin's real name is *Ogodmnpuespritis.* We shall, though, for the duration of this case history refer to him as Rubin. He is part of a small tribe, the Mogondi's. They, in turn, are connected to the Fulani Nomads, a dominant tribe in West Africa during this era.

The Mogondi's are proud, peaceful, and intelligent. They are known as the pure tribe for their links with spiritual and earthly values. Rubin is just about six-foot-tall, slim built with a constant cheeky grin on his face. He is very laid back, good natured and friendly. A feature of the tribe itself. They value life. They are not malicious people in any way, shape, or form. Though they do, protect themselves with weapons forged by their own hands. The tribe though in general are happy. They live off the land, rear their own livestock. They are clean, pure in mind and soul. They frequently wash in rocky streams six or seven times a day. Change their clothes twice.

Personally, I can see the beauty of it. The high developed mind needs to feel cleansed in every area of the body. Dutch

Missionaries have tried to convert the tribe, but to no avail. The Mogondi's laugh at this. They treat all their holy visitors well but will never succumb to another religion. Theirs is pure enough, the sun, moon, and stars. The beauty of mother earth. Their God is life itself.

Rubin is a tracker. He tracks food for the tribe, he has unusual qualities regarding it. Rubin's intuition is second to none. He is on a psychic, intuitive level that enables him to interpret the thoughts of animals, birds - even insects. I mean, this is mind blowing stuff and I do not think I have ever come across a person who does this. A man who communicates with insects - you couldn't make it up.

Rubin, though, is no ordinary man he has skills and gifts far beyond what is considered normal. He listens closely, ear to the ground and knows what a family of soldier ants are doing seventy miles away. He once saw a massive storm of locusts two hundred miles before they reached the tribal camp. It enabled the women to set net traps in the trees and get a dozen boiling pots on the go. The locusts were eaten with sweet yams and chunks of mango. How's this for an eighteenth-century stir fry?

On this particular day, Rubin leads a small party of tribal hunters. They search for food in an area not far from the coast. Rubin's mind is split. On one level, he is thinking of catching the game that they all need to eat. On the other, he has been approached to marry the Chiefs daughter **Looli.** A lot goes on in this guy's head today, more than normal. Never a good thing, not focusing on what you are doing. The hunters feel uneasy. They are too near the coastline, slightly off the chosen route. Rubin is not himself, lost in a dream, him and Looli. There you have it. A dangerous cocktail, fantasy, and judgment mixed, allowing fatal errors to unfold, completely unnoticed, all in seconds. Moments in time that turn life inside out - change it forever.

And so it was - changed in a flash. The hunters, though, armed with spears and makeshift tools were no match for the thirty or so white European slave traders. Who appeared as if from nowhere and had guns. Nets cast, heads busted, and jaws were broken. The result, though, as conclusive as any could be for the slave traders. Rubin manacled around both feet, hands tied, led away with the rest of the group. Destination, a small coastal fort serving as a slave trade drop in, drop out zone. They will stay in the fort dungeons locked up; other slaves added to the shopping list. Canoes full to the brim will then head for the trader's vessel anchored just offshore. The ship will steam full speed ahead. First to the West Indies, then on to the port of Bristol in England. Welcome, ladies and gentlemen to the white European slave trade, where business is booming - **BIG TIME!**

Rubin can't quite get his head around it. The situation he finds himself in along with others. How can he be contemplating marriage with a chief's daughter one moment? Then in the next, find himself in prison. A hell hole, thirty people, crammed into one small cell. There has to be a logical explanation, reasons; someone must appear soon and explain everything. Sadly, there is nothing to explain. Rubin is in the custody of a notorious group of people traffickers. White slavers who now lay claim to him and his group. They will ship them to Bristol docks and sell them off as *Chattel Slaves.* In other words, they will be owned for life by people they have never met.

The journey aboard the slave ship is horrendous. Conditions are disgusting, not fit for human purpose. Rubin along with other slaves, housed in tiny cages in the ships hold. They lie shackled to one another. Starved, unwashed wallowing in excrement, for some it is the end of the road. Body and spirit lie broken, and it is only a matter of time before they curl up and die.

Throughout, Rubin's dignity, poise and tactful way of thinking remain balanced. He is sad rather than hateful. Confused, but only because he does not understand the white European mentality. The tribe to whom Rubin belongs can never allow an animal to suffer like he is suffering now. So, what is the reason he continually asks of himself? How can human beings act in this way towards another man?

Dear Rubin, if I had been present, I would have gladly enlightened you. Sadly, it was not my time so I cannot offer the hand of friendship, or a grace of solace from one spiritual brother to another. If I could, though, I would sum it up in three simple words. **POWER, CONTROL, MONEY** Millions of pounds made on the back of a multitude of suffering. I often wonder just how much money is owing to black people, robbed by white traders, who unlawfully snatched freedoms and rights. It must run into billions. What is more if you take something illegally -it must be paid back under the universal law. How and when will books be balanced? Sadly, none of us has any control over what happened. And even if we did - it's too late to change it. None the less, it would be a marvelous and fair decision if the British and other governments agreed on a compensation package. The law of the universe supports it. And, there is something else. From a karma point of view, we as a nation will not move on.... until the debt is paid.

Our story continues. The date is March the 8th, 1803, and a ship fast approaches Bristol docks, a slave ship full of Black Slaves. On the quayside a hive of babbling activity gradually builds. Well-dressed men and women huddle in groups, carriages full of Toffs and their spouses arrive. It's a scene that will soon become a live chattel slave auction. Enter, Lord Freddy Forbes Froddington or as he prefers to be known - Earl of Dungeness. I can equate with the dung bit, the rest I'm not sure. What appears as the cream of British society is nothing more than people with large amounts of money, blood riddled. Tons of it, all built on a bedrock of the white European slave trade. Lord knobness, Freddy, an integral part of it.

There are five other dysfunctional members of the family to describe. Two sons, Thomas, and Breen, both gormless. Young Miss Alice, the daughter, not as stuck up like the rest and quite likable. Lady Debbie Broomfield, the woman of the household. A former society floozy who prefers bank notes to declarations of love. And finally, Dick Fixx. A once Wimpole Street prize fighter, chief bottle washer and cook. A loathsome creature with an elasticated tongue to match, reaches parts other tongues never dare to go - would make a Komodo Dragon feel inadequate.

The Forbes Froddingtons are here to choose a slave. Not just any old slave. They want a strong personality. Someone they can kick. A pliable sort who just keeps soaking up punishment. *"Treacle, up for a good kicking"* as Freddy likes to describe it. It's he who utters the first words of divine Bristol docks wisdom, "Where are the farkers, where are they Fixx. Where has this bloody boat got to?" "Will not be long now your majesticness, preparing to dock," is Fixx's cringing reply. Freddy scratches his nose and cocks his head to one side like an English bulldog with an eye on a bone. "I want the bestest and strongest farker you can find Fixx. Hear me? Single him out." Dick Fixx is now in his element, froth foams slightly around the lips. "I will get him, yer highness, I promise you. I will winkle im out by God I will. I will break im, smash the treacly boy real good and proper. You will get im on a plate, my lord."

The coiffured head of lady Debbie leans out from a carriage window. "Don't go overboard Fixx. I need him to make my tea in the morning and tend my begonias. And, I have a good oak wood spatula that I shall smack him with, on his bollox, if he gets on my nerves." She always was a bit of a determined gal that lady Debbie, never took any prisoners. Synonymous with the best looking of succulent fruit innocence - until you take a bite and discover the bile. Eventually, the slave ship docks and within a short space of time, there is an auction. It's a disgusting sight for all to see. Black men and women treated like cattle, pushed, shoved, and prodded into submissive positions while a supposed hierarchal strain of British, crème de la crème examines them. Both Lord Freddy and Fixx are in the van on this one, eager for a bargain. Finally, Rubin is spotted. First by Dick Fixx, who quickly signals his lordship to come and have a look at this superb specimen.

"Looks the part Fixx does he not? Got a strong back, and he needs it for what we have in mind." Says Lord Freddy. Dick Fixx stares longingly at Rubin then wistfully turning to his lordship utters softly. "I will av a word wiv the auctioneer your lordship. Slip im a guinea or two, we should be alright." Alright, it was, the deal being done behind closed doors so to speak. Without the hardship of having to sit in a meat market all morning sticking your fingers up every five minutes. What price Rubin went for is something of a mystery. It's not what you know but who you know, as they tend to say in certain circles of life.

Lord Freddy Forbes Froddington hated Rubin the moment they stared into each other's eyes. The reason, simple to understand. Rubin saw through him. Knew, who he was - a fraud! Let's be fair, when a man like Rubin looks into the soul of an imposter and understands who he is. The imposter knows it as well. It's as if one connects to the other, seeing their life, similar to looking through a crystal. Rubin did not hate Lord Fred. He was not capable of hating anyone so it just could not happen. And, he was still in a state of shock, finding himself in this position after living such a free life. It is at this stage by the way that Rubin gets his name. As I mentioned earlier, his real name is Ogodmnpuespritis. For some bizarre reason, Lord Freddy Froddington had it in mind that Rubin had worked on a tobacco plantation (brain dead Knobhead's with money - England was full of em). Thus developed the name. Born out of some ready rubbed tobacco theory. The surname Mind, this came from daughter Alice, who once remarked, "he looks so beautifully intense."

Time moves on and with it the life. Rubin or Rubs as the family call him has a new home after being in that dark dungeon of a boat. Doddridge Hall in the heart of the Kent countryside. It's far from a cake walk, though, and he endures several beatings at the hands of Fixx who enjoys nothing more than a good old-fashioned punch-up. Rubin, though, deals with it all. He works long and hard, and it's no sweat to him. Back on the Gold Coast, he worked twenty hours a day, enjoyed every minute. Here it is different, but the Kent countryside is fascinating, and it is not long before he has an affinity with it. Plus, he learns the English language in a matter of weeks. Courtesy of Miss Alice, who tutors him. She takes to Rubin quite readily, finding him a delightful diversion from her boring piano lessons.

Rubin's spiritual skills are manifest; they stand out no matter where he is. After a while, people in the neighbouring villages get to hear about the black slave at Doddridge Hall, who has unusual talents in all manner of things. From foretelling the future to brainwashing animals. They flock to see him; he becomes a bit of a local celebrity. There is one such occasion worth a mention.

One morning at the hall on an adjoining farmyard, a gang of pigs escape from their pigsty - all hell breaks loose. The angry hogs are running amok, snorting, snying and squealing blue murder. Dick Fixx and workers at the farm try capturing them. All to no avail, the petulant porkers getting more and more het up, it's not looking good.

Bursting on to the scene an angry Lord Freddy Froddington, on horseback with a bull whip in his hands. Starts swearing at the pigs while whipping the arse off em (to coin a phrase in his brand of colonial lingo). "Hoo-ya hoo ya stinky farkers. Get out of it, go on, go on ya buggers." Shouts his irate lordship. Dick Fixx in the meantime is definitely in a war. One of the grunting hogs trying to bite his back end and missing, latching on to his braces, pulling his pants clean off. Fixx, resembling a drunken 'Tolstoy Ballet Diva,' keeling over and lying face down in what I can only describe as super quality farmyard leftovers. Nice and fresh. Dark rich brown liquid, still with the steam on it - a treat. The pigs meanwhile are getting on top. Short of shooting them what can be done?

Rubin Mind to the rescue. He approaches Lord Fred with an idea. "Boss Freddy ya doin it wrong man - dem Pigs need the right kind of lovin. A heavy hand will not work. No, siree." Lord Freddy's face is a picture of astonishment. "What the fark would you know a treacly boy like you. The only pigs you know about are your family. Go back to your work boy or I'll whip your arse." And he well might have gone back to his work if Miss Alice had not intervened. "Father please listen to him. Rubin has incredible skills with animals," she said, a desperate look on her face. Lord Freddy looked pensive for a moment before replying. "Go on then clever dick, *'farking wankar, blood clotto'* let's see you make a damn fool of yourself." Rubin takes up a position near the rampaging pigs, crouching down on all fours he closes his eyes and makes a series of gestures to them while appearing to whistle. The result is instantaneous. The pigs stop in their tracks. Then, in single file one at a time they trot happily back into the pigsty from whence they had come and start to lie down. After this, they all fall asleep, snoring like the big fat belly porkers they undoubtedly are.

The silence that followed was unnerving. Everybody, looking at Rubin like he had the plague or something similar. I think it is important to make a point here. Not one of them in the farmyard have any idea of what Rubin has done. Lord Fred is clueless. Dick Fixx still looking like a chocolate brownie. The rest of the workforce depressed enough not to think of it. Only Miss Alice had an idea of the power in Rubin's mind, and even she could not fully understand. I believe this happens when people have no idea of spirituality, how it manifests in the life. They block it out, pretend it did not exist. In a sense, they refuse to move forward with it or give it credence.

Far from being a turning point in Rubin's life. *The Farmyard Miracle* as it became known damned him even further down the scale of evolution. At least in the eyes of Lord Freddy Forbes Froddington, who hates him even more. Rubin's work gets harder, the beatings more frequent. Dick Fixx using a leather mitten covered in sharp studs, striking his back, and leaving marks on the skin. Yet, it does not deter all and sundry visiting him, asking advice about things and events. He is fast becoming a celebrity in his own little ballpark so to speak. Even landed gentry gets to hear, making inquiries about the mysterious black man who has extraordinary control over mind and matter.

All through this stuff, Rubin has not changed one iota regarding his thinking. He is still focused, still strong in his beliefs and still has beautiful nature in how he deals with people. Even when they beat him, he bears no grudge. Those strange big eyes, *"orbs of the moon"* Miss Alice calls them, lost and bewildered. A spiritual person can never fully understand the mind of Philistines, just as they cannot understand him. The man or woman of light though will always try to make a case for people of lower dimensional behavior traits. Assist them if you like, try, and move them up the scale of evolution. Rubin Mind knows something that millions will never consider in life - we are all connected.

Five years have elapsed since Rubin first arrived at Doddridge Hall. In this time, he has taken a welter of punishment. Fierce beatings for no reason other than the color of his skin and the hate shown by both Lord Freddy and the ghastly Fixx. The physical abuse is taking its toll. Rubin looks jaded, thin; his hair is gray, and he is aging. Miss Alice, wholly dependent on him for advice and counselling, spends half her day with him and is protective of him as she can be. Though, this is not easy. The daughter now in her early twenties feels a deep bond with Rubin. She never looks on him as a slave. More like an older brother whom she is developing a deep love. She steals food, gives it to him, titbits from the kitchen. She tries to make sure he has some pleasantries in life. She reads to him, something he delights in, being read a decent book while he closes his eyes and tries to relax.

Then one day everything changes. Dick Fixx drunk as a lord decides to visit Rubin in his cabin late one Sunday evening, with the intentions of giving him another beating. Fixx drunk with alcohol but also bloated in ego, forces his way into Rubin's room and starts thrashing him with a stick. The outcome is tragic, Rubin knocked senseless, damage to kidneys and spine. It will be a month before he can walk let alone work on the estate. Miss Alice finds him covered in blood. She knows who did it but needs confirmation from Rubin himself. It came several days later when a barely audible bedridden cripple whispered the name "Feexx" through swollen, battered lips.

Alice has a plan. It's daring, but she feels she can pull it off. She wants to run away to London with Rubin. If they stay here, it will get worse, he will surely die. The beatings cannot continue and yet they will if Dick Fixx has anything to do with it. English law is changing. The slave trade abolished by an act of parliament in 1807. Though this will not be an end to slavery itself, it is a start. They are more likely to get open support than say twenty years ago. Alice knows where they can lodge in a neighbouring village with friends for two or three days. Then on to London where they can take their chance. She has a little money hidden away on the estate and with this in mind Rubin finally agrees to the plan. Before they depart, though, Miss Alice has a score to settle.

Some of the smallest insects in the world have the nastiest of bites. Rubs said it many times to Miss Alice. Let's face it he should know, back on the Gold Coast he encountered a few. Alice is only a tiny girl - but a feisty one. A girl you do not mess up. Dick Fixx will soon be a living testament to this fact. Though, at 7.00 am on a Monday morning, on horseback in his riding gear; he is not aware of it. What happens next will make him wince for many a long day. Alice went straight up to him and punched him off his horse.

"YOU FUCKING BASTARD' " yells she. "You beat an innocent man who has never harmed a fly to a pulp. Get up, hopeless cretin you." He did get up, oh he did. Only to be flattened again with another punch to the jaw. Dick keeling over like a sack of spuds and lies on the ground knocked unconscious. I mean, you can't dream this one, up can you? A slip of a girl acting like a bare-knuckled prize-fighter. *Daniel Mendoza* and his street-punching ilk would have been extremely proud.

With their luggage packed into a pony and trap, Miss Alice and Rubin leave Doddridge Hall for good. Destination, a village less than five miles away where Alice has already made arrangements with her friend to meet them. The last pathetic caption relating to this scene manifests in the shape of Lord Freddy Forbes Froddington. Caught napping by the sudden twist of events he appears in his long johns, shaking fists and swearing, running down the road shouting at the pony and trap. "You leave now 'whore' and you leave forever. Do you hear me, Alice? I will disown you, cut you off from your inheritance. You won't get anything, not a penny, **EMPTY."** Alice and Rubin do not turn back to look, infuriating his looney lordship to more vitriolic verbal. *"He's black for God's sake.* Are you listening? *He's a black nobody*, he will never achieve anything. You're ruining your life for a *nothing, a farking nothing."*

Yes, he's black, this part correct. He is black and stands tall for it, proud of his cultural roots. You Freddy boy stole them - unlawfully! As for being a nobody, you're too dense a soul to appreciate the reality. His gifts are truly spiritual and one day they will be understood to the full. Not now, though. Not while the Freddy Forbes Froddingtons run the show. The money you offer is blood money - they don't want it or need it.

The first part of Rubin Minds life draws to an end. He and Miss Alice do go to London, somewhere in the vicinity of the East End docks. It's there we lose track of them. Hopefully, they make out and find a little happiness in life. Somehow, I question it. He was ill when they left the Hall, and I wonder just how long he can survive. The life expectancy, short in these times, sanitation dismal and no health service as such. Miss Alice will do her best and try to irk an existence out for them. In a way, though, it might be better not to dwell on it. If only for the fact that it's too damn depressing for words.

What can we analyze in the first part of Rubin Minds life? Well, he does something that not a lot of people can do. He takes a massive amount of punishment, physically and mentally, yet refuses to hate his fellow man or woman. Rubin's mind throughout this karma has never hated anyone. I can tell you now, this will have a massive impact on his future life. It is going to shape him into something that ought to be a delight to behold. He has to come back with some gifted, unusual traits. In a way, he has done what a lot of yogi's and Guru's do to achieve enlightenment. He has suffered self-flagellation. Put himself through degrading and humiliating circumstances - yet refusing to lay the blame at anyone's door. He has suffered, and it is this that gets you off the wheel of karma, or, at least, part of it.

I can only surmise that when Rubin does return to his next karmic existence, it will be with enhanced awareness and ability. Because he was press-ganged into the slave trade a lot of traits did not reach their full potential. Now I am quaking in wonderment. He was so gifted in lots of ways, what will he be like when he reaches a heightened state of intuition? The essence of a super being I should think. Fifth-dimensional thinking housed in a three-dimensional body. I can see the logic of it, getting hampered by circumstances beyond your control. Cannot express or accomplish your actions in the way you desire. From a karma point of view, you physically dam up your energies and store them for another time. I made this point when I said Rubin did not reach his fullest capacity. The energies are still there, though, accruing interest at a rate of knots. When they do manifest, they will come out with a **VENGEANCE.**

In the final chapter of our story involving Rubin Mind, we see just how he got off the wheel of karma. Some of it will shock. Try not to be shaken by it, though, there are logical explanations of which I will discuss with you. The time modification process and the serialization of his karma have a massive bearing on what is to happen next regarding his future.

THE PERFECT KARMA - THE STORY OF RUBIN MIND PART 2

The year is 2030 and the place London. Rubin Mind is born again into a large family full of mixed race origins. He lives with mum, dad, and five siblings. There are four grown up boys and a girl who is five years older than him. The girls name is Alison, but they call her Alice (no surprises there), and she has a strong bond with the newly born. From the very beginning, it is plainly obvious that the child is special. He is a striking little boy, a combination of West Indian father and English mother. Blue eyes of some magnitude and beautiful high cheekbones, skin like rich brown honey. In short, he represents all that is best in Caribbean Anglo, genetic fusion.

He is a modern child, Homo Spirituous (spiritual man) born into a society that is now completely multicultural in every conceivable way. Alice, on the other hand, is old English looking stock. A dour beauty, similar to the last karma. In fact, she has not changed one bit in her looks and mannerisms. Strange, and I cannot give a logical explanation of why. You might have thought that some subtle changes could have taken place. There are none.

The family lives in a large corporation owned property quite close to Tower Hamlets in the East End of London. They are proud people who believe in hard work and productivity. Mother, Angela, is a white English Lady. His father, a Jamaican-born black Rastafarian, Michael, who runs a food franchise in the Docklands area of the city. They are all intelligent, two of the older sons have degrees. Angela is about to gain one in sociology. Beautiful people who are warm, friendly and speak impeccable English as well as two other languages. It is important to mention some of this if only to show the karmic connection between Rubin's past early life and this one.

In the previous karma on the Gold Coast, he was happy when growing, part of a gifted, organized tribe. They prided themselves on their spiritual and humane qualities. In the present karma, it is not too dissimilar. The tribal way of life swapped for a family more than equal in capabilities. He grows up a happy child, well-loved and protected.

England in the year 2030, a multicultural paradise. Many groups co-exist under the same flag, it's just difficult to keep up with them. Sadly, there is still racism. Though, not like of old. Gone are the archaic institutionalized racist attitudes of the late twentieth century. In their place, two different strains of culture blight.

Racial group preference, replacing the old white versus black scenario. There is a lot of insidious sniping about your roots, how you evolved in the UK. Then there is a violent element. Pure thuggery based on whose football team you support. Akin to this, a gang warfare culture centered around drugs. By this time, a lot of soft drugs are sold in pharmacies under strict governmental guidelines. There are, though, still a lot of dangerous ones being peddled on the streets.

Wherever Rubin goes as a young boy, Alice is not far behind him. You would expect it to be like this. The last karmic caption we had of them was one of escape. They went to London where we lost track. We will assume that they stayed together until death came knocking. I feel confident that they did but to be honest, I could not face it, the end that is. I was afraid to look at it, mainly because of how ill Rubin had become. I left it to the reader's imagination to reach a conclusion. Rubin's real name in this life is spelled Reuben, not too dissimilar to the last incarnation. His mother Angela named him after the gifted Flemish artist, *Peter Paul Rueben's.* We will keep it to Rubin, though, it is less complicated. His surname is Mynd, again though I will call him Mind. I don't like change.

Right from the outset Rubin's gifts show through, as you would expect them to. In the last life, he was brilliantly perceptive in mind, had gifts and traits far from the norm. This life is no exception, but there are obvious karmic modifications. Which we knew there would be. In the last karma, Rubin interpreted the thoughts of animals, insects. He knew their thoughts and their movements. In this life, he has transferred this ability not just to lower grade creatures, but to human beings as well. And wait for it, especially those of a lower thinking order.

Now I do not wish to be unkind or disrespectful to my fellow man. But some people do not act human. In fact, they don't even act like animals, the mindset considerably lower. The yobbo element is out there on the streets, and we cannot ignore it. Rubin has an affinity for this uncouth component, he can tame it, soothe it, and even understand the workings of it.

Desperate stuff, and you would not have thought the karmic bending for want of a better word would go down this route. But it has, the Universe knows a lot more than us - we ought not to question it. Rubin has reincarnated with fascinating skills that he will use time and time again in this life.

This is not all, though. I have already mentioned Rubin's ability to understand the mindful workings of animals and insects. It is an unusual trait and I thought this from the very outset, remarking, that I had never come across a person who had similar qualities. It was tragically cut short when people traffickers captured him, forcing him into slavery. In a way, because the ability was short-circuited, it did not reach full potential. And even though as a slave he managed to use it a few times. It could not progress to the heady heights that it was destined for.

In this karmic scenario, the Universe has righted the wrong but modified it in the strangest of ways. Rubin has come back to this world with not just the capacity to think like animals and insects - but to act like them. And in a sense, look like them. How strange is this? Let me explain, though, before you all rush to get me a strait jacket.

Rubin is a smart boy. In fact, smarter than the average Joe. Brilliant would not be an overused word to describe our Rubs. He will in the course of his young adult education amass three degrees, all with honors. Let us, though, get back to the unusual karmic qualities he possesses in this present existence. Rubin can get inside your head; he knows what you are thinking. It is a mixture of mind logic and spiritual understanding. Some of which he had in the previous karma when he worked on the Froddingtons estate. But as I already mentioned, Rubs has come back to this karma with the ability to portray himself as an animal and an insect. An insect for heaven's sake, how can anyone achieve this? I will tell you. His movements are pure instinct, and natural propulsion. He jumps like a grasshopper, works, and regiments himself like an ant, and bends himself like a sidewinder snake.

Now do not imagine for one minute that this guy can jump six foot into the air like a kangaroo. It is subtle, tantalizing, and does not stand out in the beginning. The Universe has equipped him with little bendy twists and turns, that you hardly notice until they are upon you. Even I cannot quite get a grip on it, such a remarkable quality that he has. Rubin can manifest himself like a rubber man. He feints and jinks like liquid plastic on stilts. Is in front of you and then behind you, all seemingly in one precise movement. He has two eyes like most humans. Yet, they resemble a centipede. They are everywhere, all over you. The dude never misses a thing.

The funny thing is, though, when he carries off some of these wacky antics - he actually looks the part. In the sense of assumes the pose and shape of whoever he is trying to imitate. I cannot think of anyone who is like a centipede, but there you have it. All packaged in the neatest of formats. It's mind blowing stuff.

In fact, it is the most amazing one-man circus of events that you could ever see. It will, though, be instrumental in providing Rubin with a lucrative form of wealth-massing in a few years from now. The very beginnings of this we will witness soon, and I shall explain how his skills and natural talents shape him for the future. In the last karma, Rubin took an enormous amount of punishment. Sadistic beatings delivered from the hand of the maniac Dick Fixx. He died under this vibration, a victim, a man that the whole world and his dog see coming - and want to abuse.

As I have stated many times, though, the Universe does not desert you. If it needs to step in to help you on your karmic pathway, it will do so. In this instance, Rubin brings back his perpetual minder and confidante. Alice, the lady who ended up caring for him in the last karma. She is his bodyguard. Though to be fair, later, he will not need one, but she has an inbred fixation to look after him. And similar to the last life, no one tells her what to do.

When Rubin is eight years old, an event happens at his junior school that will determine his future, at least in the present karma. His intelligence is way above his age group, and the school put him in a class two grades higher than normal. He shares a good rapport with the other pupils, but two boys dislike him intensely. There is no reason, except that of possible resentment to his popularity. One boy is of Somali culture; his name is Dannu. The other lad is Karl, a white English boy.

They are not awful people, just school bullies who love to dominate a weaker link. Rubs singled out as the link, a guy they feel they can push around and frighten. Rubin is not afraid of them, far from it. He understands their mentality, gets inside both heads, and studies them. The two boys feel that because he is so open minded and friendly, he is easy meat for a bit of hard and swift punishment.

One particular late afternoon, Rubin stays over class time, talking for more than half an hour with Mike Jackson, his math's teacher. Together they ponder over a complicated equation that Rubin is mastering. Eventually, saying goodbye to Mr. Jackson, he walks out of school and into the playground, where he intends taking a shortcut, leading to a bus stop and eventually home. Out of nothing suddenly appear Dannu and Karl, the two school bullies. It is Karl who speaks first. "Well, well, well. What have we got here? Rubin, the brain of Britain. Licking teachers arse yeah?" Before Rubin can answer Dannu leaps into the conversation. "Bout time we taught you a fuckin lesson arse-licker." Rubin, calmer than a mill pond, looks into Dannu's eyes - and knows what is on its way.

As Dannu lunges forward, fist raised, he does a little hop, skip, and a twizzle. Leaving Dannu to slap thin air, Rubin ending up behind him with arms folded. I am at odds to describe it. He looked a cross between a frog doing a Saint Vitus dance, and an ice skater pulling off a triple lutz. Dannu though is a picture of mental bewilderment. This, in turn, causes angry Karl to rush headlong at Rubin, fists flailing in frustration. It is a pointless gesture. Rubs, parries the blows effortlessly with his briefcase, before imitating himself into a man-made rubber snake. His body bends to the side, allowing Karl to run through him and fall flat on his face - knocking himself out in the process. The whole thing a comic strip, Groucho Marx could not have done it any better. Our boy Rubin dismantles both school bullies without doing anything, he does not touch them in any way. I can only describe it as smack in the gob stuff. Flip the lid baby!

What happens next. Well, Rubin helps Karl to his feet and sits him down on a small garden wall adjoining the playground area. Delving into his briefcase he pulls out a bottle of spring water, giving it to Karl to drink. Dannu, who seems to be in a trance while all this is going on suddenly, discovers his vocal chords. "Your weird man and crazy. Yeah, crazy spasmo. I ain't sticking around here." With that, he makes a bolt for it. Karl is not in a bad way but cut his lip when he fell. Rubs walks over to the school cloakrooms, finds some water to clean him up. When he returns, Karl has gone, run off with his briefcase. Which goes to show, you may have the ability to penetrate the mind of a philistine - not necessarily be able to change it.

In the brief time that all of this took place. There was an onlooker. Yes, somebody saw it, every detail. The person was Mike Jackson Rubin's teacher. He could see the whole scenario through corridor windows overlooking the school playground. Right from the outset, Mr. Jackson had an urge to stop what he thought was a minor scuffle. But something held him back. He was riveted to the spot, a combination of fascination and jaw-dropping awe. Plus, it happened so fast and I doubt whether he would have made any impact. Anyway, he sees what happens and cannot believe his eyes. Rubin's lightning-fast movements, the body curve, and bend, it mesmerized him.

Mike Jackson is fit in both body and mind. He served in the Army where he learned amongst other things, the noble art of boxing. Jackson calls on Rubin later that night and speaks to his parents. On the teacher's recommendation, it is agreed by all that Rubin joins a gym. There he can learn the pugilistic artistry of the fight game. Fighting for a living, who would have thought it.

Yes, who would have thought it possible. From a study though of his karma, I will say it is a necessity. In the last life, He took a multitude of beatings. So many in fact, they became ingrained in the future life blueprint. Fundamentally, he is tied to a game of defense and attack, even though it is not his thing. This will not make him aggressive or a bully boy. Rubin is too developed to go down this line. The simple truth of it is, the Universe has stepped in to equip him with all the necessary tools that will solve his karmic problem. Rubs cannot do it on his own, this is obvious.

Once more, it exemplifies what I have been trying to force feed into you, from the beginning. If you have issues doing it on your Jack Jones - the Universe gets involved. You get help, we all need it one way or another. Rubin, up at the crack of dawn, down to the gymnasium where he is fast learning the noble art. Alice is delighted. Think of it, though, she would be. The sister has reincarnated to this present life as his protector and minder.

From a karmic point of view Alice is a bit of an enigma, she worries me slightly. Her attitude is far more belligerent than the last life. She is feistier and more antagonistic, especially towards white English born people with acidity in their voice. If Rubin goes into a store and an English guy talks a little bit hoity-toity to him, she wants to bang him out. In a way, her karma is going down this little side route where I don't feel she should be. Like I have said, though, there is no way of fully understanding how karmic traits develop within each individual. The soul energy is a law unto itself and will manifest in the way that it wants. No way should anyone try to interfere in any shape or form.

By the time, Rubin is nineteen his life is beginning to gear up. His education complete, and he has three degrees of some standing. One a master's in philosophy. As a student of the noble art, he is fast becoming the real deal. Several fights have gone his way with little or no effort and his confidence is growing. The guy's ability to dodge punches is unbelievable. You have to see it yourself to understand how spectacular it looks. The punches that get through are caught effortlessly on the gloves. Because he is so spiritual, so developed in mind, he has set criteria regarding how he feels about the fight game.

Rubin never throws a serious punch to the head. He relies on a jab to score points. It's more of a flick, hardly touches the skin, yet deadly efficient. Especially where the judges are concerned. He is a model of consistency, a future champion.

Alice is one of his corner men, but also his part-time manager. At this stage not so important. Later, though, she may prove to be a handicap, her attitude becoming more aggressive by the day. It is odd to think of it being so. Because he suffered so much in his last life one might have thought Rubin would have the aggression - there is none. Making it even more of an oddball scenario. A fighter with no fire in his belly, just the pure ability to box his opponent into total submission. I have never seen this, even the greatest, *Muhammad Ali* got angry at times. Yet, Alice the sister who was his companion and minder in the last Karma possesses all the brutality under the sun. A graphic example of this coming up next.

An individual's karma always follows them. We should all know this by now. Even though Rubin is not well known, trouble always looks for him. They all want to hand him a beating. It goes with the karmic territory so to speak. One particular Saturday afternoon Rubin and Alice decide to attend a football match, watch their favorite team the Arsenal. Standing in the bar of a North London pub they enjoy a pre-match drink. The atmosphere is a pleasant one. Multicultural tongues resonate, glasses chinking away, excited banter and the sound of *Baba O' Riley* being belted out by *The Who.*

Across the room, two guys study the pair intently. One is white, English, the other white, Eastern European looking. Perhaps from the Balkan states but it is hard to judge in this atmosphere. Rubin knows something is not quite normal. He sees them clocking him from the corner of his eye, must be the centipede in him. Either way, all the signals are read, understanding the intentions of both. Alice is not so aware; she rambles on obliviously about the next up and coming fight he is to compete in.

Sauntering over to the bar with stupid looking grins on their faces the two suspect individuals lean on the counter, stare full on into Rubin's' eyes. It is the Eastern European one who speaks. " friend thinks he knows you, thought he recognized you." Rubin grinned as good-natured as he always does. "A case of mistaken identity guys." With this, the English looking one seized the initiative. "Not really pal, you look like a drug dealer. In fact, I thought you were the seedy little bastard due to meet us half an hour ago." Rubs chuckling to himself. He knows where this is leading, he will enjoy the challenge of philosophically brainwashing both. Sending them on their way enlightened. "Here for the game, two great teams should be a cracking match," He says enjoying his lemonade shandy. The Eastern European guy is now in his element. "Match! The only fuckin match mate is your face and my ass. **THATS A GOOD MATCH.**"

Under normal circumstances left alone without interference. The situation is more than likely to go Rubin's way. Already he is tinkering in the guy's mind. Sadly, some things never reach a satisfactory conclusion. The Eastern European took a step back, a gesture of defiance maybe. Or, just needing a little room in preparation for his next move. We will never know the reason. At this juncture Alice, sandwiching herself between Rubin, facing the mouthy yobbo, punches him right on his nose. She then flattens him again, a stiff uppercut to the jaw. In fact, she punches his lights out faster than Rubs ever does to anyone in his fights. Over in seconds, knocked out cold.

It is a similar scenario to how she clobbered Dick Fixx in the previous karma. The other Gobshite, well he just stood there and pissed his pantaloons. Yes, literally, bladdered out all five pints of lager he had just consumed. The lunatics asylum, you have to be there to understand.

How Rubs and co-managed to get out of this remains a mystery. They did, and pretty quick. The Eastern European guy and his mate did not want any further trouble. Both ran off once sanity had been restored. Rubin and Alice asked to leave the pub. They obliged and were glad to. After all, it could have been damaging publicity even at this stage of the game. Rubin, though, is definitely not pleased with Alice and lets her know about it. "Why did you do it? Why? I can handle myself. That guy would have been eating out of my hand." Alice looked pensive, slightly put out. "Your ridiculously soft always were. I saw the hate in his face. I stepped in to save you." She paused and went on. "We should have held our ground, let them call the police. Nothing would have happened to me. They verbally abused you and were going to attack you, self-defence on my part, for you; *We could have sued the trash.*"

Rubin pushing hands through hair, sighing despondently. "When will you learn? Beating someone to death is not the answer. Neither is taking them to court every five minutes on trumped up race motives, just because you cannot get your own way. We need to rise above it, the mindset needs change." Looking intently at her he continues. "Evolving mind and soul. This is the way forward. *Dr. King* believed in it, and he was right. Get inside the essential nature of the beast - and change it. Progress Alice, it's called progress bring out the guilt within them, get them to face the shame." A distinct silence follows before she offers the right of reply.

"You will never achieve what you are trying to do, never. You can get inside a person's head but will not change their viewpoint. Your weak Rubin always will be. You won't rise above anything. And, you will never be world champion. **YOU'RE NOT THE KILLER YOU NEED TO BE."** With this said, she storms off leaving him to ponder the vitriolic acid in her words.

Two years pass. Rubin, in his early twenties, he has fought many times. Won all his fights, always in a similar style. He boxes his opponent off his feet, does not punch much, it is pure trickery and art. He is seen by his peers in the game as the most exciting new prospect England has ever had. Certainly, regarding winning a world title fight outright. Before he attempts this, though, he must win the British middleweight crown and establish himself as a genuine world contender.

The title is currently held by *Mitch Muffler Andrews*, a white English born guy who lives and boxes out of West Bromwich in the West Midlands. Andrews is a skilled fighter with a rock solid punch, most of his fights settled quickly by knockout. Like Rubin, he has never lost a fight and represents a difficult foe to conquer. Mitch Andrews has no respect or liking for Rubin, looking on him as a novelty and a joke. He calls him Mr. Lucky the man with no punch. The fight is due to take place just before Christmas. Before we talk about the fight, we should take time out and evaluate Rubin's karmic progress so far.

He has come back to this life in the way I imagined he would. Though, there are slight discrepancies. The life has definitely got easier, nothing resembling *a slave trade karma.* He still has incredible skills about sensing the future. He knows what's coming, short term at least. The bit about how he acts like an animal, an insect is a surprise. Though, to see it inaction, the way he builds it into his fight routine you can definitely make a case for it.

Alice though, well she is the enigma. The time has modified her karma, bringing her back as an agitated young thing. I mean, she had some spunk in the last life but now - she is at times unmanageable. In fact, you would think she was the fighter and Rubin the support act. In many ways, perhaps he should be looking after her and not the other way around. I can only think that the anger she endured in the previous life has followed her back with a vengeance.

In a way, this is the lesson about karma that we all have to be wary. If a trait, a feeling of emotion becomes so ingrained in one's life. Then in the future circumstances, it can manifest as something completely out of control. A dark demon, festering the mind, looking for a way to get out. Don't go there, don't even think about it. Try and control the emotions, err on the side of caution.

The time for the fight with Mitch Andrews draws near. Awareness of it everywhere and the newspapers full of it. They have nicknamed Rubin, *Bendy Boy,* due to the way he can dodge punches. The fight will take place at the NEC just outside of Birmingham. The whole family will be there supporting him, and Alice will be in his corner. She has taken on the full role of Rubin's manager which should be of no surprise to anyone.

Mitch Andrews is a big head. His ego fueled by the number of knockouts he has achieved and overblown write ups in the Daily News. At the weigh in Andrews verbally attacks Rubin and manager Alice. "You're going down in one Bendy Boy," says he, contempt written all over his face. Looking at Alice, he leers gropingly before continuing his piece. "Shall we order the ambulance now miss? Or perhaps make it a hearse, cos I'm gonna kill him."

Alice would have flattened the idiot there and then if Rubin had not gently held her arm and restrained her. Looking at Andrews square in the eyes he says. "We shall see on the night. Bring plenty of support Mitch - you will need it." Mitch Andrews looked taken back by this as if he did not expect anyone to question his authoritative tone. "They don't call me 'Muffler' for nothing. The silent assassin that's who I am, I muffle em out. Bring on the body bags." After the customary 'staring each other out' procedure, both boxers got weighed and answered a few questions for the press before departing.

The fight for the British title was the most one-sided affair you will ever see. In a packed NEC arena, Rubin entirely dominated Mitch Muffler Andrews. In fact, Andrews only landed two punches of any worth. A shot to the head which glanced Rubin's hair as he quickly ducked it. The other, an intended body blow, blocked before it could make its mark. Rubin, on the other hand, weaved and dived his way around the ring, landing shots to the body, scoring every time. They were not killer blows; they did not have to be. By the time, both boxers reached round eight of a scheduled twelve. Rubin was streets ahead on points. Round eight was to be the deciding round.

Mitch Andrews, by now the most frustrated man on the planet came out of his corner guard well up. He ran at Rubin almost full tilt to finish the fight. With gravity-defying moves, the Bendy Boy kind of dragged his body to the side, allowing poor Andrews to miss him altogether and end up going headfirst straight through the ropes. There he lay on the deck completely knocked gonzo - *good night Vienna.*

The developed soul knows its own karmic pathway. This is always so. When minds reach a high state of development. They as individuals become aware of the path they must tread for the future. Rubin Mind is now British Middleweight Champion and has a *Lonsdale Belt* to prove it. He must progress further and fight for the world title. The title is held by a man named Richard Fitzwilliam's, nicknamed Mr. Fix. He is none other than the reincarnated soul of Dick Fixx and wait for it - he is black!

This will surprise a lot of you, yet it shouldn't. In the previous karma, Dick Fixx hated black people so much that he became one in the future. The hate, developing into obsession, eventually turning into its opposite - changing to love. In a strange way, he was a white man who longed to be in a black man's body. You can find a clue relating to this in the earlier part of Rubin's story, see if you can spot it.

As a boxer, Mr. Fix, as we shall call him, is a perfect punching machine. He boxes out of New Orleans in the USA, ruling the world middleweight division for over five years. He is mean, nasty, and as yet unbeaten. It's not hard to see how Dick Fixx would have developed into this guy. In the previous karma, Fixx loved beating people to a pulp. The karmic trait now reaches its fullest expression in the present incarnation.

The modified Mr. Fix is a killing machine of some standing. The Fix has a manager. A funny little man with piggy eyes and a pot belly. He calls himself *Fred Freeze* and wears a striped suit and a bowler hat. He is a white American businessman who was born in New York. Enter, the reincarnated soul of Lord Freddy Forbes

Froddington.

Like Alice, Fred has not physically changed from the previous karma. There are no reasons as to why, and I cannot give any. Continued negotiation between Alice and Fred Freeze eventually produce a contract to bring Rubin to the United States. There he will fight Mr. Fix for the world title. The newspapers and media are calling it the fight of the century. The Fix man who beats his opponents to pulp against Mr. Bendy, the man you cannot hit. A match of brute force versus astute cunning and skill. The fight is a sell out as soon as tickets go on sale. Rubin knows that this encounter with Mr. Fix is part of his destiny. He senses it like I said earlier, the developed soul knows its own karma, or nearly so.

Thus, when Rubin and Alice first meet Mr. Fix and Fred Freeze, there is a distinct feeling of uneasiness. Rubin is aware that this man who he must step in the ring with soon is part of his karmic development, or degradation depending on how you view it. Rubs will know in an inherent sense that this man was in his previous life. He cannot remember it, will have no chance of doing so. But the soul knows that this is big. This is different, to the point of being life changing. The mere fact Rubin thinks on these lines shows the advanced stage of development within.

At this point, I will talk a little more about how Rubin and Alice first meet Mr. Fix and Fred Freeze. The meeting serves to highlight subtle ways karma works in your life. At the first public press conference in New York, some weeks before the fight, they finally set eyes on each other. Mr. Fix as soon as he sees Rubs hates him. Not surprising this, he hated him in the previous karma, nothing has changed. Rubin, on the other hand, does not feel anything. He does not hate this man; he bears him no malice. He knows, though, a lot is riding on this fight. Not just materially. He knows there is something that has to be settled between them, it's deeper than the average boxing match grudge.

Mr. Fix would love to punch Rubin there and then in the press conference. Something is holding him back. That something is

Alice, she stands between him and a third world war. A strange unease comes over him when he looks at her. He is wary, and so he ought to be. The beating she handed him in the last life still resonates at a soul level.

Fred freeze, well he has taken quite a shine to Alice. He touches her arm at every conceivable opportunity, keeps making strange remarks. Freeze seems paranoid about the agreement he has signed regarding the upcoming fight. He runs behind her harping on about various clauses that are in the contract. "Alice, you must give us seven working days' notice of any changes made to the contract we have. The document made between us will be null and void if you don't. You will lose money if this is not adhered to. If you do not comply with this, you will not be paid." To the naked eye, it looks a simple case of a fussy old man frightened to death of being ripped off. At karma level, though, this is where we left them in the last life. Lord Freddy chasing the pony and trap, going on about money and inheritance. Karma repeats, I say it all the time.

The year is 2054 and a boxing match of some consequence is about to take place. The location, New York, Madison Square Gardens, known now as purely, *The Garden.* The crowd packs the venue to the maximum, hardly a seat in the house. Enter the Gladiators first up is the current champion, Richard Fitzwilliam's. Or as we know him, Mr. Fix. He enters the ring to a cavalcade of cheers and boos. The music plays to the tune of *Bobby Bland, I pity the fool.* An apt choice, considering the emotions being shown by Mr. Fix - none whatsoever. It is then the turn of Rubin Mind, better known as the Bendy Boy. He enters the ring to massive cheers and the sound of *Sonny Boy Williamson singing, Cool Disposition.* An equally apt choice if old Bendy can live up to it. Finally, the scene is set. 'The greatest show on earth ready to begin.'

MC Michael Murray starts the proceedings. "Ladies and gentlemen. On behalf of ITC International in conjunction with Fred Freeze promotions, we present a night of world championship boxing. A middleweight fight sponsored by Universal boxing associations. For the UBA middleweight title of the world. Introducing in the red corner, boxing out of New Orleans in the United States of America, and weighing in at 158 pounds. He is the current holder of the belt. Middleweight Champion of the World, Richard, Mr. Fix, Weeeeeeeeeeliams." Once more, cheers and boos mixed. "And, in the blue corner from Tower Hamlets in London, England, weighing in at 156 pounds. He is the challenger, Rubin, Bendy Boy, Myyyyyyyyyyynd. Your referee for the fight is Dr. Dan Dorkins from Chicago."

The bell sounds, round one of a twelve rounder is underway. Mr. Fix tries to make it a quick knockout, coming out of his corner all guns blazing. Rubin dodges the first four punches easy. Then catches the next two squarely on the gloves before ducking slightly to the right, flicking out two quick stinging jabs to the side of his opponents face. In Mr. Fix's mind, they probably felt like the ping of an elastic band. No weight behind them but they scored points. The Fix is amazed at how quick his adversary responds he realizes that the fight is not going to be a pushover.

Time for the world champ to try a little brainwashing. "where you really from boy? I mean, yer not black nor white, kinda treacly looking if you ask me." All of this gets whispered into Rubin's ear, treacle gets a mention! Where have we heard this before? Rubs, having none of it, knows what the champ is trying to do. He backs away, ignores the hype. Two more quick jabs to the lower chin then the bell rings. End of round one.

Insects are hardly powerful creatures. Well not in the singular sense. They can, though, be vicious in their own particular way. You only have to study nature to see some truth in this. I suppose a good example would be a soldier ant. Tiny, diligent, annoying and bites. Stick a few of them together and the problem is multiple. In a sense, this sums up our Rubin. His punches, if you can call them that, resemble the flick of an ant's mandible - they sting. Put a few of them together and in the collective sense they damage - draw blood. By the time we reach round four, this is beginning to happen. Mr. Fix's face is becoming red, scratched looking. The energy is still there, but he is more than frustrated at the fact that he hasn't landed a severe blow. It's no good being able to punch like a streetfighter if you're only punching the air. Once more he tries the brainwashing plan. "Is this the best yer can do rubber-boy? A million girls are watching ya perform. They must be thinking, this here rubber man. Take us all day to find his dick, let alone ride on it. Ha, ha, ha, fight me, baby, **FIGHT ME.**" Before Rubin can think, the bell sounds. Round four is history.

Three more rounds pass, the fight becoming a procession. World champion, Richard Fitzwilliam's better known as Mr. Fix is being taken apart. Not in the normal way, though. Rubin Bendy Boy Mind is cutting him to pieces with jabbing, razor-like flicks of the wrist. They sting the champs face like an army of ants chopping into a caterpillar. Blood shows on cheeks and chin like tiny rivulets of red ink. Try as he may, the champ cannot get near his adversary. The Bendy Boy skipping, jinking, dancing, and ducking all seemingly in one coordinated move. Mr. Fix can hardly see him let alone throw punches at the guy. And what is more relevant, he is getting tired. The exhaustion beginning to show, the strain of the night telling.

When the bell goes to signal round seven is over, Fix's corner shows their frustration. "C'mon champ, you're not boxing. Nail him at his own game get the jab going." In reply, the Fix man finds it hard to speak. "Can't reach the *motherfucker,* can't get hold of him. He's like a cloud - 'Son of a Bitch' like punching dust. I fuck the blood clot if can get him" Fred Freeze looks a worried man. "Well you God darned better get hold of him fast, or we lose this fight."

They will lose the fight. If this is not too premature a statement to make. It is round nine and Mr. Fix is making no impression or progress regarding points scoring. Try as he may he cannot get near our Rubs. Karma-wise, the logic of this is straightforward enough. In the last life he beat him up at will, no resistance offered. The Universe has given Rubin every defensive skill and strategy to be competitive in this karma. The Fix is wasting his time, you cannot fight the universal law, no matter how good you think you are. As we go further into round nine, the current if i can is more and more frustrated. He is not being beaten to death the way he tends to do with opponents. It is subtle, jabbing flicks, sustained over a period of time with no let-up. His face, puffy and red, held together with sticks of adrenalin. He is being annoyed into submission.

There is a knock down towards the end of the round. Fix in his desperation to hit Rubin rushes headlong into a blinding, flicking jab to the eye. He loses balance and falls, enough for referee *Dr. Dan Dorkins* to delay proceedings and send Rubin to a neutral corner. The Fix man is angry, he vents it. "I slipped; he didn't hit me. The motherfucker ain't got near me. **THE BLOOD CLOT NEVER TOUCHED ME - C'MON I SLIPPED."** Referee Dorkins is having none of it. "Mandatory count buddy, neutral corner if you will. Now box on." They did, but the bell sounded soon after. Rubin's corner excited as schoolkids. Alice is full of praise. "You got him, you got him, Rubin. Just keep it up your miles ahead. Three more rounds and you are world champion."

It is round ten of the scheduled twelve and something strange is about to happen. Something that neither of these fighters will ever have considered, in twenty lifetimes, let alone one or two. It's hard to explain. I will do my best, though. The round is following a similar pattern to the others. Mr. Fix, frustrated and losing decisively, cannot get in a blow. Rubin pins him on the ropes jabbing that stinging flick into his face. He is covered in blood, cannot see properly and is worn out to the point of collapse. The stinging flick jabs, resembling a few ants gnawing away with their mandibles, have now become a swarm of killer stings. To Fix, it feels like the torture of a million cuts.

The crowd is beginning to sense victory, already there are shouts to stop the fight. **THEN IT HAPPENS!** A bizarre series of mystifying moments that cannot fully be explained. To Rubin, it was if the whole fight ground down to a slow-motion pace. He could hear the crowd baying in the background, their shouts, distant and barely audible. The Fix was in front of him, his guard down offering no defense. His mouth was open, and he looked as if he was trying to say something.

Rubin got close up to him so as to hear. "I'm sorry," says Fix. "What!" says Rubin. "Sorry, for what?" The champs blood soaked lips mouth a reply. "Past, present, not considering it possible I could be on the wrong side. Not understanding what it's like to lose. I ain't never lost, don't know what it's like, seeing it from a loser's viewpoint. The man pays - I do the job." Rubin looked puzzled. "What about the future," He said. Mr. Fix tried to laugh. "Future, I ain't got no future, never did have. It's yours. You take it Bendy Boy - see it as me, your my future. You're in my place now."

It was precisely at this moment that Rubin fully understood. The futility of his past life and the ridiculous irony of the present. It's as if he had a karmic premonition. He sees it and understands. Only he is in control of this priceless information, only he can act upon it. Rubin knows that people like Mr. Fix are not the real perpetrators of any crime, racial or otherwise. They are machines with minds to go with it, doing as told. The real power lies within a chosen few. The controlling elitist element that determines progress or regression in this life. Before, though, he could think more the bell rang signaling the end of round ten. Rubin goes back to his corner knowing the path he has to tread.

The Bendy Boys corner is going bonkers, the crowd shouts his name, "Rubs, Rubs, Rubs." Alice is the first one to speak. "It's yours, baby, you got it good, Mr. World Champion Man." Rubin, silent, pensive he does not say a word. Just before the Timekeeper's bell is due to ring, he drops the bomb. "I'm through. I'm not going out there. I quit." The two seconds looked stunned. Alice with a desperate look on her face starts shouting. "Don't be stupid. Streets ahead, you are streets ahead. Get out there and finish him. Nail the bastard, Rubin. **NAIL HIM!"**

His head bowed forward in a posture of defeat, the man who stands on the brink of history is a force spent. No longer has the heart for it, nor sees the necessity of continuing. He just sits on his stool and stares into dark space. When the bell goes for round eleven, Rubin Mind remains in his corner. The fight is over!

Alice is frantic. She speaks to referee Dorkins and after a few seconds of heated debate manages to get a stay of execution lasting one minute. Almost crying with frustration she tries one last time to motivate her man. "For pity's sake, Rubin get out there. This is our chance, what we dreamed about. Please don't blow it. Please, Please." There is no chance of reprieve, he refuses to budge, stays on his stool, and is ultimately disqualified.

The crowd is stunned into silence. Only momentarily, once they grasp the situation, there are boos and shouts of derision. Everyone is of the opinion the fight has been fixed. In the Fitzwilliam's camp, there is obvious joy and celebration. To be fair, though, he is not lauding it. He embraces Rubin, head down looking at the ground. In fact, at one point he actually slips on the canvas and assumes a pose, looking like he is praying for forgiveness at Rubin's feet. The Fix will never fight again and within two months he will retire, a broken man.

The real truth will never come out of why the finest middleweight boxing challenger to grace a world championship fight, quit on his stool. In the press the next day, the camp divides into jointed conclusions. One the obvious, the fight had indeed been rigged. The other, a little more sophisticated. It reported that Rubin had been so intent on destroying Mr. Fix, he had burnt himself out completely. *Bendy Boy runs out of steam'* says one daily. *Champ elect in a fix - he burns out on his stool*, says another. Either way, it is universally accepted that Rubin Minds career is over and that no one in boxing will touch him again.

The loneliest place in the Universe - a dressing room at three am on a Sunday morning. In it sits a fighter, who has just lost a world title fight, a contest he was winning hands down. Rubin Mind languishes in solitude and reflects on the biggest non-event in his career. Suddenly, there is a knock on the door and in walks Alice. After closing the door behind her, she stands in the middle of the room staring at him for over two minutes.

Then with an apparent venom in her voice starts speaking. **"YOU 'FUCKING RETARD.'** You sick, pathetic breed. Had to do it didn't you. Rubin Mind the great philosophical no-hoper. The man whose idiotic viewpoint of a karmic utopia or whatever he wants to call it, allows him to throw away the biggest night of his career." She paused and then continued. "You're finished, washed up. I'm finished, you ruined my life." Rubin's face, a contorted jigsaw of obvious pain. He looked at her in a way that begged she stop the verbal onslaught. She didn't, it continued. "You're on your own now. I can't stand you. In fact, I hate you and I mean it. Get out of my space, pathetic loser. Get out of my life.

'BASTARD OF A BREED' THAT IS YOU!"

Eyes, partially closed, blocking the pain of murderous words. He hardly noticed her deft litheness of movement, as she came right up to him, face to face, full on. Which is why he was not prepared for what happened next. In a move, that had to be seen to be believed. Alice hit him with a sledgehammer punch, right in the middle of his face, just above the nose, and into the forehead. The blow so hard it made a thwacking noise. He fell down in a heap and lay there, prostrate, gone with the fairies, out like a Chinese lantern. With one last disdainful glance as he lay in dreamland with his mouth open. She stole away into the night, quietly closing the door behind her as she left.

Sometimes, you cannot explain things to your own mind. Like waking from a deep sleep, wondering how the hell you arrived, the God darned mess surrounding you. For those who don't know Rubin, it might seem an easier enough choice to lay the blame on others. He won't do it, not his style. Alice has physically abused, and racially degraded him - her own brother! It matters not, he makes a case for it within himself and moves on. The long night, though, has definitely left a calling card. So it's hardly surprising to find our battered hero idling down West 43rd Street, looking for a bar where he can drink in the early hours of the morning. He finds one, there are many in this part of Manhattan.

New Yorkers can be the nicest of people. No one bothers Rubin as he sits with a coffee and a large bottle of cognac. In fact, they hardly notice him. Which says a lot for their discretion, or the fact that they just want to get on with their own lives, leave others to theirs. As Rubin sits, sipping his drink at the bar, fidgeting with dark glasses hiding part of his face, he is aware of someone sitting next to him. He looks up to see a beautiful girl smiling. She has long dark hair and looks American, a hint of Eurasian skin tone and fabulous eyes. "Hello," she says. "Hi," says Rubin in reply. He has never seen her before, yet there is something familiar about her. "Do I know you?" "I've got a feeling you don't," smiles she, "But I know you. You were in that fight tonight," she gazes openly at him. Rubin looked down at his glass - "I lost that fight." A slight pause before she responds. "No, you didn't, you gave it away. I think you're amazingly generous. Hey, you must have felt sorry for the guy." He felt a touch embarrassed, not sure what to say - so she says it for him. "Don't worry honey, we all lose one way or another, part of the *Zippo lifestyle.*" The way it came over, so innocent, makes him laugh. Which proves infectious, she starts laughing too.

They talk well into the night. Eventually, she has to go, getting up from her barstool, she hands him a small box of complimentary hotel matches. "Call me." Rubin looking longingly at her. "I will, but hey, what's your name. I don't know your name." "My name is *Lulu.*" With that, she turns around and leaves, looking back once to wave at him.

New York City, 8.00 am in the morning. The world's busiest metropolis is grinding out a daily routine. The noise of the city evident, cars honking horns, people hustling and bustling, all looking to get to where they are going. Ambling his way in the direction of the Hudson River docks area, Rubin peruses in his mind all the recent events that have had so drastic an effect on him. Where will he go now and what will he do? Some questions still have to be answered when returning to England. He will, of course, face stinging criticism, especially from the press. For now, though, all he can think about is the girl he has just been talking to in a bar. Rubin muses over her deeply. Lulu, the name rings a bell, definitely. *Where have I seen her before*, he thinks to himself. *She certainly seemed familiar - so easy to talk with.*

Up in the sky, a welcome burst of sun filters through the clouds. Intermingling with early morning mist that is rising off the Hudson. Soon, the long lingering haze will disperse, and a day of decency will descend upon the Big Apple. In the background, against the urban noise of traffic and people, you can hear the horns of the tugboats chugging up and down the river. Rubin, his senses, keen and lively, his mind beginning to focus once more. He closes his eyes and suddenly - knows everything that is happening in Manhattan. There is a newfound spring in his walk and a feeling of optimism about the future. He thinks to himself, perhaps, life had to work out in this way. Maybe, this is where it is destined to end. Maybe...

FINALE

A sad conclusion, or a good one? Who knows, only Rubin can tell us. Whatever way you look at it, though, I do not think it ended in the way we all thought it would. In a sense, we the readers might have imagined a nicer closure to the story, in particular between Rubin and Alice. But the message I have gone overboard to preach in this book - you can never truly understand the individual workings of a soul. Especially, their karma. It's a fascinating area, the mindset of individuals, how they exercise free will. One thing I am sure of after evaluating Rubin's performance in the course of this story. He gets off the never- ending karmic merry-go-round. I will list my reasons for believing it.

He did not hate. He went through a lot of things where he might have done. We, as sane free minded individuals could possibly make a case for him if he had ended up despising people. After all, he had his freedom and rights taken away from him, illegally! It was not seen like this during that era. But the truth is, the universal law was violated. Yet, this man did not ever at any time use the blame game, perhaps only on himself for being in a position that allowed him to be exploited. He certainly did not hold anything against his fellow man or woman. I am pretty sure in myself that this is one of the hardest things to do in the whole of the Universe - not hating people at some point in your life. **I CAN'T DO IT.**

Rubin never allows the hate emotion to take him over. A lot of people have difficulty in banishing this trait. You only have to talk to a mother or father, who have just had their son, daughter, murdered to put this into perspective. But what I am saying is: If we can forgive, rather than hate. Then it will go a long way to releasing us from the future burden of our own individual karmic circumstances.

He bore no malice, moved on quickly. Important this, Rubin never allows the poison to grow within him. Always, he wants to move into the future leave the past behind. It's kind of like a fifth-dimensional thinking process. If you can master it, then it becomes a great asset for you. By not dwelling on the bitterness of the past, you lessen the chance of a negative future. In a sense, you do not invite any negativity in. Can I (me) master this process? Well, I'm trying, learning like the rest of us, we are all in it together. None of us are perfect or we would not be here!

He took multiple beatings, experienced intense emotional pain. I can hear the gasps as you spit your coffee out while reading this bit. No one in the world would be expected to take this kind of punishment just so they can ascend to a higher life. If you think of it, though, this is what developed *Yogi's, Guru's and Spiritual Masters* put themselves through to achieve enlightenment. In a way, getting off the karmic wheel is similar. It's all about the physical and emotional pain, feeling it, sustaining it within ourselves, getting something from it, good or bad. Of course, most of us experience it gradually, on a daily basis, the highs, and the lows so to speak. In a way, Rubin got it all in one go, spanned over two lifetimes. You can see why some people give up.

He turned his back on materialism. This was probably the biggest sacrifice Rubin made in the two lives. He was a stone throw away from landing an enormous fortune. If Rubs had just stayed with it, beaten Mr. Fix, which was a foregone conclusion. He would have collected millions. Could any of us have done this? I doubt it. Could I have done it? No, I would have knocked the Fix out, taken the cheque - and legged it. And, to be practical over this, I do not feel one would need to go as far as Rubin to prove the point. He did, which is fine. Mere mortals, though have practical needs, economic nightmares that require constant attentions. The analogy, though, is there! If you can separate the money from the principles, ethics, keep them in perspective, you will not go far wrong. Separating the two keeps you on the right side of the fence.

Finally, he was spiritual. He tried to see the higher side of life. Rubin was a gifted person; he was naturally intuitive. Some of it inherent I am sure. The tribal atmosphere he grew up in on the Gold Coast, a sensitive one. We cannot all aspire to this ability. But, if we as individual souls can only think about it, embrace it to ourselves and have some faith in it. Then we can progress further than we imagine. Sometimes, this is all you need, a touch of enthusiasm, a modicum of flair, the will to keep at it. Ten percent ability, ninety percent hard work and reflection -

IT ZINGS.

I hope you enjoyed the book - I enjoyed writing it for you, for me, for all of us - Anthony.

END

ANTHONY J MEAD

BOOKS BY THIS AUTHOR

The New Age Karma Handbook

This book will teach you about karma - how it really works. There is priceless information regarding the most important aspects of the karmic process. Especially the the last part of life leading up to death. Find out how the Universe modifies past life traits and fits them into your present. There are various story lines full of information. Including an explanation of why some people come back with severe difficulties -physical, mental and emotional.
The book is soul food and should be treated as such.

Anthony J Mead.

BOOKS BY THIS AUTHOR

Simplified I Ching - The Magic Tortoise Oracle

The author explains how to read the symbols of the I Ching and fit them into every day life. There is a totally new, innovative, way of constructing the 64 hexagrams.

This is so easy to understand you can formulate questions in your head and make the hexagrams while walking to the shops. The Magic Tortoise Oracle is like a guide to help you through the day - keep you safe and put your mind at rest.

Anthony J Mead

BOOKS BY THIS AUTHOR

The Incredible Doctor Zoom - Casebook Files

Paul Zoom and his wife Jean live in Stamford, Lincs, they run a clinic. Not a normal clinic, one that concentrates on the paranormal, the mystic and the downright unearthly.

Empty Souls who refuse to move on but would rather takeover anothers mind. Druids who want their pagan powers restored. Evil Souls who plan a Casino heist - take control by brainwashing the staff.

Only Paul Zoom and his team can solve the issues - read on and learn how they do it.

BOOKS BY THIS AUTHOR

Parable Of A Rich Man

23: Then Jesus said to His disciples, "Truly I tell you, it is hard for a rich man to enter the kingdom of heaven. 24: Again I tell you, it is easier for a camel to pass through the eye of a needle than for a rich man to enter the kingdom of God."

What does this parable mean? - does it mean if you make a lot of money you cannot go to the higher life? NO! It means that a person with great wealth finds it hard to leave the earth and their money behind them. Anyone can ascend - Adolf Hitler could do it or has done it. No one can stop a soul from reaching the higher dimensions.

Yes, Jesus was right it is easier to liquify a camel and pass it through the eye of a needle - than for a wealthy man to renounce his earthly millions and leave for a life that they havn't got a clue about. Or whats more to the point, can't buy their way into. There are many souls clinging to the earth plane. They are frightened to go and leave what they think is theirs - but in reality it isn't theirs and never will be. Reincarnate from heaven to earth or from earth to earth YOUR CHOICE.

Printed in Great Britain
by Amazon

83773768R00089